Accolades for...

The Believer's Basics Handbook

"Feast at the table Sadira Davis has created for you! The *Believer's Basics Handbook* is packed with rich revelation and deep wells of truth from the word of God. Each chapter is foundational to every believer and holds keys for us to be positioned for kingdom living. With every turning of a page, you can literally hear the call to come up higher. Get ready for a heart transformation!"

Susan Cheatham
Susan Cheatham Ministries
Scmfire.org

"Prophetess Sadira Davis has done an excellent job of putting together all the foundational scriptures needed for all believers. This book is a much- needed resource for the body of Christ. I am so glad that this has been written. Going forward I will use this tool as I continue to disciple."

Sylvia J. Stout, Apostle Spirit of Christ Coalition International
Melbourne, Florida

"Reading *The Believer's Basics Handbook*, I was impressed with the layout and developmental plan for new believers. The introduction outlines the rationale and opportunities for growth through believership, discipleship, and kingship. The book progresses to explain Sadira's initial action and provides a plan to assist in *reframing* the believer's mindset. The book is well-written. I believe it will be a helpful tool for believers to grow with clear direction. Each chapter made me want to read the next chapter. I believe the book will serve as a useful training manual to those who struggle with their identity and purpose and provides them with steps to becoming a disciple in Christ."

In Him, an Ambassador in bonds
Apostle Ulysses Tuff The Way, The Truth, & The Life
Christian Center,
Inc. Decatur, Georgia

"The *Believer's Basics Handbook* is for every believer that desires to grow and develop in the things of God. In this book, Prophetess Sadira helps to provide the believer with knowledge and understanding of key foundational truths. There is solid content and information sure to benefit many as they journey in their Christ walk."

Apostles Emmanuel & Belinda Allen Breakthrough Life
Church

Glendale, Arizona

"The *Believer's Basic Handbook* is packed with foundational and revelatory truths that are applicable to the life of every believer. I wish I had a book like this when I was young in the Lord and budding as a young minister. This is not just a book for you to read once. This is a book that you should have on hand to not only read again but also to use as a reference for your daily walk with God. I want to encourage senior leaders to get this book into the hands of their new members, new converts, and ministerial teams. I love how Sadira highlights what should be considered vital to our Christian walk.

And to be quite honest, much of what she outlines and describes in this book, though it's biblically based, it's also lost to the current generation.

Things like faith, the kingdom, the gifts of the spirit, intimacy with God, money, ministry gifts, the church, spiritual fathering, and so much more still seem to be foreign concepts to many in the church today. We can't grow up until we have a solid foundation. You can't build a structure on a faulty foundation. In a generation where everyone desires quick promotion and the fame of the pulpit, I've come to discover that a vast majority of these people can't even articulate the basics of what's written in this book. You need this for your foundation. You need this for your knowledge and understanding. Herein lies the basics for Christian discipleship. You need this for your life.

Dr. Lionel M. Blair, Sr. Founder and President:

Imperial Kingdom Apostolic Movement Global

(IKAM Global) Newport News, Virginia

The
BELIEVER's BASICs
HANDBOOK

Building Blocks for a Solid Foundation
in Christ and Kingdom Living

SADIRA DAVIS

STAR LAMB
PRESS

The Believer's Basics Handbook:
Building Blocks for a Solid Foundation in Christ and Kingdom Living

StarLamb Press 1343 W. Glenmere Dr. Chandler, AZ 85224
www.sadiradavis.com

Identifiers: ISBN 978-1-7365842-0-0 (ebook) | ISBN 978-1-7365842-1-7 (paperback) | ISBN 978-1-7365842-2-4 (hardcover)

The Library of Congress has cataloged the trade paperback edition as follows: LCCN: 2021903794 (print)

Printed in the United States of America
©2021 by Sadira Davis

Table of Contents

PREFACE

I n the 21 st century, with technological advancement at an all-time high, information being at our fingertips and approximately 900 printed English translations of the Bible, it would seem that "believers" would be more effective, full of power works, and *more* spiritually grounded than the early church thousands of years ago. Disappointingly, it just is not the case. After many years of ministry and travel across the United States and abroad, it is safe to say that too many believers do *not* have a "sure foundation (2Tim. 2:19; 1Cor. 3:11-14)." What I mean is that the most rudimentary elements of living godly (kingly), as an heir of God and joint heirs with Jesus, are either not present, not active, or incomplete in the lives of most professed Christians or "believers" (Heb. 5:11-14; Rom 8:17). Many do not know how to sufficiently pray or hear God's voice; how to study the Bible nor have a good understanding of kingdom living verses present day churchdom living. They can't articulate why Jesus came, beyond quoting John 3:16, and they most often have no idea what life after accepting him is supposed to look like.

At this point, you may think that I am totally out of order to make these assertions that appear "judgmental" and even presumptive to some degree. "How do you know what's in the hearts of people" or "how can you imply people don't really know God or how to live godly" are some of the questions I'm sure will arise in the minds of those reading this. I want to assure you that my statements are not rash or presumptuous but are provable, and most importantly biblically based. Jesus tells us in Matthew 7:15-23 the realities of "trees" being observable and their origin or nature being distinguishable by its "fruit:" what it produces. He is specifically speaking of prophets, those established to be deliverers of God's will, plan, and purposes, but it is applicable to *all* mankind as prophets were considered the standard bearers. He also tells us "*TO judge*" in John 7:24, but to be sure to do it righteously, which means with the standards of God in focus; not judging superficially or out of our opinions or social (cultural) standards (John 7:24; Lev.19:15). I challenge you to take this journey with me through the following chapters and to assess and see if I'm telling the truth according to the word of God. Everything that I will present will corroborate with scripture *and* align with God's plans and purposes for mankind. So, buckle up, take out your favorite Bible and get ready for a journey of fortification in *truth*.

In the simplest terms I am going to share who Jesus is, why he came, how he lived, and how we should live if we are true followers of him: disciples. God only works in order (legally), and in justice (righteousness/impartiality/equity) and is the establisher of the highest legal justice system ever. Therefore, nothing that He does will ever violate the very order He has set. His word, the Bible, is the law of the Lord and is the believer's law (Psalm 1:2). He is a just and righteous God and there is not any "shadiness" (variance, inconsistency, or "shadow of turning") in Him according to James 1:17.

You will leave this learning platform with sound doctrine of Jesus Christ and the ability to live in victory over the ever-present enemy (Satan) and worldly systems. You will also learn how to "reign" as a super-natural king as God intended in the beginning at Eden.

Sadira Davis

King & Priest (Rev. 1:6) Chandler, Arizona, 2020.

INTRODUCTION

"The Situation"

It was the beginning of man's years as heirs of God (little gods). Mankind was created and placed in their first training ground; a region called Eden to recreate the environment through domination and reign like their Father and creator God (Gen. 1:28). God ordered them to "subdue" and bring every living thing into subjection to their kingly authority. It was Genesis, a beginning, and as with every beginning there's an order of things and there are boundaries established. We see the Moon being ordered to govern the night and the Sun the day and the firmament and waters having a boundary (Gen. 1:3-19). Everything life-bearing is ordered to produce after its own kind; the law of procreation and seed time and harvest being ordered to operate in the earth.

Recognize that seeds are not just the little objects that produce fruit or plant life that you imagine when you hear the word but are the origin of *anything* which essentially can

1

potentially continue indefinitely. Words, thoughts, actions and such are all types of seeds along with the hosts of seeds that we are most familiar with. For example, we see in Proverbs 6:19 it speaks of one who "soweth [seeds] of discord among brethren." So, we understand that seeds are entities possessing gestational ability. God himself sowed countless seeds with anticipation for manifold harvests. He created the earth, animals, and every single living creature with perpetuating capabilities built in; every tree for decoration and food (Gen. 2:9; 1:29-30), and mankind as a "seed" or carrier of himself (Gen. 1:26-28; 2:7). He created the "Garden of Eden" as a domain conducive for unending fellowship with him, reproduction of life and all things good, as well as to be a "piece of heaven" on earth; "a kingdom" for man to govern (Gen. 2:8; 1:28). This region in the earth was established that man was legally made to have "dominion" kingship and rulership over, including everything in it; through inheritance given by the Father.

We must understand that kingdoms are either established by or seized by kings. Historically, we can also see some kings or queens being grafted into a royal lineage through the covenant of marriage.

2

For example, Esther who was a Jew, became a royal queen by marrying King Ahasuerus (Esther 2:17). Therefore, when one wants to become a royal or king, he must obtain it through lineage through covenant or by taking possession of the kingdom by seizing it *from* the king(s) that are the present ruler using force; any means of deception or capture or by death (killing/destroying) them.

God established an earthly kingdom in the Garden of Eden and made Adam and Eve to be the royal leaders over it. They were explicitly commanded to "subdue it [the earth]" AND "have dominion" over EVERY living thing in it (Gen. 1:28). By Genesis chapter 3, in walks the "subtle serpent (Gen. 3:1)" with seeds (instruments of perpetuation) ready to make "covenant" and procreate with the newly set order in the earth: humanity. He, Satan, strategically wooed Eve by captivating her mind. He first offered Eve seeds of doubt; both in her identity as a royal leader and in the instruction to eat and reproduce life and good *only*. He then gave her the seeds of evil and death in which she did eat and gave her husband to eat; technically and legally "covenanting" with her (them: Adam & Eve). This resulted in them being inseminated with death. In essence, Satan both covenanted with them *and* poisoned and killed them, therefore legally seizing the kingdom given to man by God in the earth (Gen. 3:13; 3:1-24). This act ushered in the reign of death, evil, and rebellion (disobedience to the sovereign rule and orders of God). Hence, we see the first deaths: Adam and Eve spiritually die (distanced from God – Gen. 3:9; 3:23-24) and physically die "returned to dust" (Gen. 3:19); plus, the innocent animal's death which was killed to provide "coats of skins [to] clothe [cover] them [both physically and spiritually] (Gen. 3:21)." Herein, we also see the institution of the blood sacrifice; innocent blood being shed as atonement (reparation or payment) for guilt (sin; behavior repulsive or offensive to God and his holiness) (Gen. 3:13-21). Keep in mind that seeds perpetuate continually in their genetic properties. So, when Eve "did eat" of that which Satan offered her, she became "pregnant" with all he fed her: lies, doubt, self-esteem issues, identity crisis, rebellion, etc... Additionally, the practice of guilt being satisfied with innocent blood is made an order legally ushered into the earth as a seed and becomes a perpetual practice. The "DNA" of man is polluted /altered/ mutated from this point forward, causing ALL men thereafter being "born in sin and shaped in iniquity (Ps. 51:5; Eph. 2:3; Rom. 5:12; Gen 6:5).

Now as "subtle" and witty as the enemy was, righteousness is still superior. Therefore, our righteous king, who is even more strategic regained the kingdom with superior methods. In due course, "King Jesus" enters the earthly realm through immaculate conception as a "pure seed" (free from man's sinful lineage) legally "born of water [of the womb] and of spirit (John 3:5)" to legally seize the kingdom back. It was a most unlikely entrance (birth) and an even more unsuspecting death and resurrection that totally and openly shamed the devil and legally reclaimed the reign over the kingdom of Eden in the earth; Eden (represents the spiritual place of unending fellowship with the Father/ veil rent), and the souls of men. Colossians 2:15 (NLT) says, "In this way, he disarmed the spiritual rulers and authorities. He shamed them publicly by his victory over them on the cross." Now all believers have redemption (from the curse of sin death and the law) through Jesus' blood and are translated into the kingdom of Christ and light (out of the power/dominion of Satan and darkness) according to Col. 1:13-14, Eph. 1:7, Titus 2:14, Gal.

3:13, 4:5; Rom. 3:23-25, 1Peter 1:18-19, Heb. 9:12, Rev. 1:5-6, Rev. 5:9. Most importantly it was his sinless (spotless) life that made him a qualified "innocent blood" sacrifice.

5

This legal seizure and then full payment made it possible for each person who confesses Jesus Christ as their Lord and personal savior to be "redeemed" (reclaimed with full compensation being satisfied for their sins) and liberated back into a place of kingdom rulership in the earth and full access to the Father, Heaven, and all the privileges therein.

In the following chapters I will cover the basics of this new life: believership (being born again/inducted into faith), discipleship (training in followship), and kingship (obedient sonship) which together hold the [fundamentals] of a born-again/new creature life and what is needed for a solid foundation in Christ and for true kingdom living and reign while on the earth.

PART ONE:

ENTRANCE TO SALVATION:
BELIEVERSHIP

Chapter 1

What Is A Believer?

As in times past, many people attest to being "believers", but the term is used so loosely that we need to delve into a deeper discussion centered on this ideology of believership. The literal word believers only appear twice in the entire Bible, with both instances in the New Testament (NT) (Acts 5:14 & 1Ti 4:12). Believers were most often identified in the NT scriptures as disciples (committed students; learners; followers of the truth), the elect, or saints who were growing and were "fruit bearing." What I mean is that naturally there is a process of seeds being sown, impregnation or germination followed by a gestational time and voila "fruit" or whatever the "after its own kind" product (Gen. 1:11, 24-25). So, when a disciple has observed, studied, and believed the things that he has been taught by his teacher, and then, by faith (conviction of belief), puts them to practice; he will *show* that he is reborn

9

or "born-again" and an actual *believer* by the manifestation of fruit, works, etc. 2 Timothy 2:2 (AMP) says, "The things [the doctrine, the precepts, the admonitions, the sum of my ministry] which you have heard me teach in the presence of many witnesses, entrust [as a treasure/a seed] to reliable and faithful men who will also be capable and qualified to teach others [and will reproduce after this kind]. This scripture fully captures the life and process of a *born-again* "believer." People "believe" in and have belief about a lot of things and that's why we have to emphasize that we are talking about the *"born-again"* believer. We do the title no justice if we are not bearing the actual fruit of what we say we believe. So, if you say you are a Christian, but you do not emulate Christ, responding as a "new [reborn] creature," that is a disservice, and it brings shame and dishonor to God. It also brings question to the validity of your believership.

The word believer in terms of definition is noted on Lexicon.com as "a person who believes that a specified thing is effective, proper, or desirable; [and/or] an adherent of a particular religion [faith]." Strong's definition notes a believer as "one who [has] kept his plighted faith, worthy of trust; that can be relied on; [and] who is [fully] convinced that Jesus is the Messiah and author of salvation" and

Thayer defines it as, "trusty, faithful; persons who show themselves faithful in the transaction of business, the execution of commands, or the discharge of official duties." This last definition is explicit in that one *MUST* believe to be an executor of business and commands of the Lord and written word of God. Therefore, one cannot truly "commit to faithful men who will do the same (2Tim.2:2 paraphrased) unless they actually have *first* believed and become reborn (changed) themselves. Mark 16:17 is also a prime example of "believership." It duly states that "these signs shall follow them that *believe*; in my name shall they cast out devils; they shall speak with new tongues. They shall take up serpents; and if they drink any deadly thing, it shall not hurt them; they shall lay hands on the sick, and they shall recover (Mark 16:17-18 KJV)." We must accept that you cannot and will not produce anything that you don't believe possible; that's not a seed *in you*.

Is it safe to say that we have an innumerable amount of those that profess Christ as Lord and attest to being "born-again believers" but they in fact lack belief if there is no manifestation (fruit) of that belief? I mean would you honestly believe someone if they presented an apple tree to you and tried to convince you that it was an orange tree?

Yet, most "believers" are trying to make the world believe they are something that yet lacks the fruit of their testimony as *born-again Christian believers*. Now of course we do not like the fact that someone would imply that you or I, my righteous friend, do not believe the way we may think. Remember in Matthew 7:16-17 KJV Jesus himself tells us to "know them by their fruits... [because]... every good tree bringeth forth good fruit; BUT every corrupt tree bringeth forth evil fruit." It further implies impossibility for a tree to be tricky. It *cannot* be corrupt and bring forth good fruit or vice versa. It is impossible. A tree can *only* produce based on its core nature and the seeds within it. Therefore, believers *believe* and respond to life from that core of believership. When we come into a full understanding of the role and work of Christ Jesus, and how *that* is the foundation of our belief system, we will begin to actually bear the fruits of that tree. We will begin to move by the Spirit executing the will of the Lord in the earth, bringing the kingdom of God to a dark and lawless generation just like Christ did.

In simplest terms, we will portray what is our culture by what we believe, what we eat, how we dress, how we speak and how we live. Merriam- Webster defines culture as "the customary beliefs, social forms and material traits of a racial, religious, or social group; *also* : the characteristic features of everyday existence (such as diversions or a way of life) shared by people in a place or time **b** : the set of shared attitudes, values, goals, and practices that characterizes an institution or organization **c** : the set of values, conventions, or social practices associated with a particular field, activity, or societal characteristic." If we are to represent the culture of the kingdom of God or the culture of Christ, we must do as Christ did. He readily and blatantly stated that, "he was here to do the will of His father (John 4:34; John 5:3o; John 6:38)" that "He *only* did what He saw His Father do (John 8:28; John 5:19)" and that those who were of God (His sisters and brothers) "were [*only*] those who [also] do the will of God. (Mark 3:35)." Our attestation of being a born-again believer must align with that of Christ *if* that is upon whom we have believed. Believers are to show forth belief [faith/conviction] in their everyday lives. In Romans 1:17, Galatians 3:11 and Hebrews 10:38 we are told that "the just [those who are justified by faith/belief in Christ] shall live [survive and thrive] *by faith* and "if any man draws back [releases their faith/belief] that the Lord has no pleasure in this retraction of confidence in Him."

My prayer is that from this chapter of "What is a

Believer" you will be compelled to do some extensive examination of yourself. The bible tells us in 2Cor. 13:5 (AMP) "**Examine** and **test** and **evaluate** *your own selves* to see whether you are holding to your faith [committed to your conviction born-again life in Christ] and showing the proper fruits of it. Test and prove yourselves [your position]. Do you not yourselves realize and know [thoroughly by an ever-increasing experience] that Jesus Christ [anointed one/gift giver/empowerer] is in you – unless you are [counterfeits] disapproved on trial and rejected?" Check your life, check your tree, your roots; check your fruit and determine if you are truly reflecting Christ and the Kingdom culture. Or do you look like the world you live in and the current culture of it? Selah.

CHAPTER 2

FAITH THE 1ST FOUNDATION

Faith can be explained in several ways. We will look at the secular definition, the biblical references and discuss the revelation the Lord has given for a full understanding. First let's take a look at the Merriam-Webster definition of faith. It has a few ... faith means:

1a: allegiance to duty or a person: loyalty

b (1) : fidelity to one's promises (2) : sincerity of intentions **2a** (1) : belief and trust in and loyalty to God (2) : belief in the traditional doctrines of a religion **b** (1) : firm belief in something for which there is no proof (2) : complete trust **3**: something that is believed especially with strong conviction; *especially*: a system of religious beliefs

Now in the Bible the word is only mentioned in the Old Testament two times; in Deuteronomy 32:20 and Habakkuk 2:4. In both scriptures the Strong's Hebrew translation is "emuwn" or "emuwnah" which means in Deuteronomy "established, that is figuratively, trusty; also, abstractly trustworthiness: faithfulness, trusting, truth." In Habakkuk 2:4, the meaning "literally firmness; figuratively security; moral fidelity: faith, set office, stability, steady, truly, truth, verily."

All the definitions thus far identify faith as a noun as something concrete or as an adjective describing the validity of its concreteness. Hebrews 11:1 (KJV) describes it as "the substance of things hoped for, the evidence of things not seen." This now leads me to the "revealed" understanding of faith. Faith is the "currency of the Kingdom" and the actual means by which we transact business in both the heavenly and earthly realms from the spirit. Everything we see in the natural comes from the "unseen" or "spirit realm" according to Hebrews 11:3 (AMP). "By faith [that is, with an inherent trust and enduring confidence in the power, wisdom and goodness of God] we understand that the worlds (universe, ages) were framed *and* created [formed, put in order, and equipped for their intended purpose] by the word of God, *so that what is seen was not made out of things which are visible* (Heb. 11:3)." This means that everything we see came from the spirit realm.

Faith, a conviction concrete enough to use, as a means to manifest both physical things and spiritual things, is a criterion to walk in covenant with God. In Hebrew 11:6, it tells us that "without faith it is impossible to please him [God]: for he that cometh to God must believe that he is [existent now/alive], and that he is a rewarder of them that diligently seek him [as such]." The entire 11th chapter of Hebrews goes on to extrapolate the value and consistence of faith's exceptional effectiveness in the lives of those who utilize it to operate in God's will through their journey of life in the earth.

Hebrews 11: 2-40 (KJV)..."For *by it* [faith] the elders obtained a good report.

³ *Through faith* we understand that the worlds were framed by the word of God, so that things which are seen were not made of things which do appear.

⁴ *By faith* Abel offered unto God a more excellent sacrifice than Cain, by which he obtained witness that he was righteous, God testifying of his gifts: and by it he being dead yet speaketh.

⁵ *By faith* Enoch was translated that he should not see death; and was not found, because God had translated him:

for before his translation he had this testimony, that he pleased God.

6 But *without faith it is impossible to please him*: for he that cometh to God must believe that he is, and that he is a rewarder of them that diligently seek him.

7 *By faith* Noah, being warned of God of things not seen as yet, moved with fear, prepared an ark to the saving of his house; by the which he condemned the world, and became heir of the righteousness which is *by faith*.

8 *By faith* Abraham, when he was called to go out into a place which he should after receive for an inheritance, obeyed; and he went out, not knowing whither he went.

9 *By faith* he sojourned in the land of promise, as in a strange country, dwelling in tabernacles with Isaac and Jacob, the heirs with him of the same promise:

10 For he looked for a city which hath foundations, whose builder and maker is God.

11 *Through faith,* Sara herself received strength to conceive seed and was delivered of a child when she was past age because she judged him faithful who had promised.

12 Therefore sprang there even of one and him as good

as dead, so many as the stars of the sky in multitude and as the sand which is by the sea shore innumerable.

13 These all died *in faith*, not having received the promises, but having seen them afar off and were persuaded of them; embraced them and confessed that they were strangers and pilgrims on the earth.

14 For they that say such things declare plainly that they seek a country.

15 And truly, if they had been mindful of that country from whence they came out, they might have had opportunity to have returned.

16 But now they desire a better country, that is, a-heavenly one: wherefore God is not ashamed to be called their God: for he hath prepared for them a city.

17 *By faith,* Abraham, when he was tried, offered up Isaac: and he that had received the promises offered up his only begotten son,

18 Of whom it was said, That in Isaac shall thy seed be called:

19 Accounting that God was able to raise him up, even from the dead; from whence also he received him in a figure.

20 *By faith,* Isaac blessed Jacob and Esau concerning things to come.

21 *By faith Jacob*, when he was a dying, blessed both the sons of Joseph; and worshipped, leaning upon the top of his staff.

22 *By faith* Joseph, when he died, made mention of the departing of the children of Israel; and gave commandment concerning his bones.

23 *By faith* Moses, when he was born, was hid three months of his parents, because they saw he was a proper child; they were not afraid of the king's commandment.

24 *By faith* Moses, when he was come to years, refused to be called the son of Pharaoh's daughter;

25 Choosing rather to suffer affliction with the people of God than to enjoy the pleasures of sin for a season;

26 Esteeming the reproach of Christ greater riches than the treasures in Egypt: for he had respect unto the recompence of the reward.

27 *By faith* he forsook Egypt, not fearing the wrath of the king: for he endured, as seeing him who is invisible.

28 *Through faith* he kept the Passover and the sprinkling of blood, lest he that destroyed the firstborn should touch them.

29 *By faith* they passed through the Red sea as by dry land: which the Egyptians assaying to do were drowned.

30 *By faith* the walls of Jericho fell down after they were compassed about seven days.

31 *By faith* the harlot Rahab perished not with them that believed not when she had received the spies with peace.

32 And what shall I more say? For the time would fail me to tell of Gedeon and of Barak, and of Samson, and of Jephthae; of David also, and Samuel, and of the prophets:

33 Who *through faith* subdued kingdoms, wrought righteousness, obtained promises, stopped the mouths of lions.

34 Quenched the violence of fire, escaped the edge of the sword, out of weakness were made strong, waxed valiant in fight, turned to flight the armies of the aliens.

35 Women received their dead raised to life again: and

others were tortured, not accepting deliverance; that they might obtain a better resurrection:

³⁶ And others had trial of cruel mockings and scourgings, yea, moreover of bonds and imprisonment:

³⁷ They were stoned, they were sawed asunder, were tempted, were slain with the sword: they wandered about in sheepskins and goatskins; being destitute, afflicted, tormented;

³⁸ (Of whom the world was not worthy:) they wandered in deserts and in mountains, and in dens and caves of the earth.

³⁹ And ***these all, having obtained a good report through faith,*** received not the promise:

⁴⁰ God having provided some better thing for us, that they without us should not be made perfect. (BibleGateway KJV)"

Faith empowers the believer. Faith acts as a type of portal for things to pass from the spirit realm into the natural realm: strength, courage, power, capability, resources, armies of angels, you name it. All these believers from history model for us the utilization of faith for everyday situations, some great and some smaller, but none not achievable *by* and *through* faith. We must choose to exercise our faith in any and every situation without reservation but with full confidence of its effectiveness. God wants his kingdom to manifest here in the ways that it is operational in heaven. We must realize it is our duty as believers to be vehicles for such display.

PART TWO:

CONVERSION: FOUNDATIONAL DISCIPLESHIP I

CHAPTER 3

BUILDING INTIMACY THROUGH PRAYER

When most people think of intimacy, they think of romantic relationships; they may even further isolate it to mean a sexual encounter. The truth is that intimacy *is* a relationship word, but it is by no means limited to a romantic relationship. However, it does denote a deep level of relating (communing). According to Dictionary.com, intimacy means, "the state of being intimate; a close, familiar, and usually affectionate or loving personal relationship with another person or group; a close association with or detailed knowledge or deep understanding of a place, subject, period of history, etc.; an act or expression serving as a token of familiarity, affection, or the like; an amorously familiar act; liberty; sexual intercourse; the quality of being comfortable, warm, or familiar."

When I speak of "building intimacy through prayer" I am in fact speaking of specifically a closeness, a familiarity, an affectionate and loving personal relationship with the Lord. Prayer becomes the vehicle as would conversations with one in the natural that we would seek to get more acquainted with. In both the Old Testament (Deut. 6:5) and New Testament (Mark 12:30; Mt. 22:37; Luke 10:27) the scriptures tell us to "Love the Lord your God with all your heart, with all your soul, and with all your strength or mind." This is a commandment spoken to us to define the expected context of the relationship with the Lord; a loving or more specifically an *intimate* one. The same way you build an intimate relationship with someone in the natural is the same way you build one with God (the Father, the Lord Jesus, and the Holy Spirit). You must spend time in frequent open (naked; no holds barred: unrestrained) communing. Prayer and worship are what we use for this. Prayer is merely a means of communing with God; sharing of intimate thoughts or feelings to build and strengthen the relationship. Prayer also involves us posturing ourselves to receive communication *from* Him as well. Let us look and see how this is carried out throughout the scriptures.

In the very beginning it is established that God had a

standard visiting or meeting time with Adam and Eve in the Garden. Genesis 3: 8 says "And they heard the sound of the Lord God walking *in the cool of the day*, and Adam and his wife hid themselves..." which lets us know this was a regular meeting and they were now not wanting to meet because they had shame from their sin. In Genesis 12:1 the Lord *tells* Abram to "leave his country and people and go to the land that He (God) will show him (paraphrased)." From here going forward, we see many scriptures of the Lord speaking to or communing with man and vice versa. Prayers. It is essential to any intimate relationship, especially at its inception; that there are *regularly scheduled* interactions. Yet intimate communication is required throughout the life of that same relationship if it is to be sustained.

In the New Testament we see Jesus Christ, our chief example, leading us to show that it is of the utmost importance to "steal away" and have frequent communion with the Father in order to accomplish our life's purposes. In Hebrews 5:7 it tells us "in the days of His flesh, He offered up both prayers and supplications with loud crying and tears to the One able to save Him from death; He was heard because of His piety (devoutness, holiness, saintliness)." Throughout the Gospels he is seen often going away to the mountains or wilderness by himself to pray or with the disciples nearby (Mt. 14:23, 26:42-44; Luke 5:16, 6:12, 9:18, 11:1, 22:32; Mark 6:46, 1:35, 14:32-39, John 17:1-25). Here's a few of them:

☐ Mt. 14:23 (KJV) "And when he had sent the multitudes away, **he went up** into a mountain **apart to pray**: and when the evening was come, **he was there alone**."

☐ Luke 5:16 (KJV) "And **he withdrew himself**☐nto the wilderness, **and prayed**.

☐ Luke 6:12 (KJV) "And it came to pass in those days, that **he went** out into a mountain **to pray, and continued all night in prayer to God**.

☐ Luke 11:1 (KJV) "And it came to pass, that, as **he was praying in a certain place**, when he ceased, one of his disciples said unto him, Lord, teach us to pray, as John also taught his disciples."

This must become our practice if we intend to have a strong relationship with God, and to live a successful born-again life. Like the disciples in the above scripture, we must want him to teach us to pray by following his examples and by talking with him about *it* and other things. Time in prayer is the key component to a healthy intimate relationship with the Lord. Period.

Maybe you are having a challenging time praying because you feel unequipped. Maybe your difficulty is due to the fact that you do not visibly see God, so you feel ridiculous having a conversation with someone that is invisible. Well let me share with you the model that Jesus gave the disciples and that is a suitable place for everyone to use when they are getting started on a journey of intimacy through prayer. In both Matt. 6:5-11 & Luke 11:1-4 Jesus spells it out very plainly how to approach our Father in Heaven. Let's take a look:

Matthew 6:5-13 (KJV)

"And when thou prayest, thou shalt not be as the hypocrites are: for they love to pray standing in the synagogues and in the corners of the streets, that they may be seen of men. Verily I say unto you, They have their reward.

6 But thou, when thou prayest, enter into thy closet, and when thou hast shut thy door, pray to thy Father which is in secret; and thy Father which seeth in secret shall reward thee openly.

⁷ But when ye pray, use not vain repetitions, as the heathen do: for they think that they shall be heard for their much speaking.

⁸ Be not ye therefore like unto them: for your Father knoweth what things ye have need of, before ye ask him.

⁹ *After this manner* therefore *pray ye*: Our Father which art in heaven, Hallowed be thy name.

¹⁰ Thy kingdom come, Thy will be done in earth, as it is in heaven.

¹¹ Give us this day our daily bread.

¹² And forgive us our debts, as we forgive our debtors.

¹³ And lead us not into temptation, but deliver us from evil: For thine is the kingdom, and the power, and the glory, forever. Amen". Now let us break it down verse by verse to get an even clearer understanding.

In verses 5-6, Jesus is instructing us not to try and use prayer as a means for public applause or to convince people that we are righteous. God rejects us when we are in pride.

Seek God in private "in your closet" and build intimacy and relationship that you can cherish and be excited about. Building a solid relationship will produce more than a superficial one on any given day. When you have built a strong solid relationship, it will be identifiable by others when they see you publicly because you are being changed and assuming God's nature from your private intimate interactions. It is the same way people notice how married couples seem to grow to act like one another; some would even to look alike. It's the intimacy that does this. Intimacy opens us up, in the highest level of vulnerability, to receive and be changed. There is a song that I love sung by Steffany Gretzinger that expresses this very happening. The song says, "The more I seek you, the more I find you; the more I find you, the more I love you..." A deep loving relationship will form as you pursue God through prayer and it will make you more like him: loving. Love is a bridge to allow encounters with God. Therefore the charge is high to love; we are commanded to do it and master it. The more you fall in love with Him, the more you submit to Him and the more He is given permission to be seen in and through you.

In verses 7-8, Jesus continues to tell us not to make prayer "ritualistic" by merely repeating phrases, clichés, or other verbiage we have heard muttered by others who often are only saying the things they say to impress others or to try to get something from God. He knows what we need and will provide for us, but He wants intimacy with us more than anything. How would you feel if you met someone and each time you have an encounter with them they are just saying a certain set of phrases repeatedly and then they commence to asking you for something? You would probably think they were crazy, but you would definitely feel like they were just trying to use you instead of being genuinely interested in becoming your friend or lover. Well, the Lord has feelings and is disinterested in this approach as well.

Now in verses 9-13 is the "meat" of the matter. This is where Jesus tells us step-by-step what to do to gain the kind of relationship that He has with the Father. He says to first acknowledge Him: "*Our Father* which is in heaven, hallowed be thy name..." Hallowing is to honor as holy; it is you recognizing his greatness, his holiness, his rank as Father Lord Leader. It is a bestowment of respect and love. After you have honored and loved Him up really good, you acknowledge your agreement and alignment with *his* will and purposes for your very earthly residence; "[*His*] *kingdom* to *come* and be executed here on earth as it is in heaven." This indicates that you are truly his son/daughter. A righteous heir of a throne will uphold the righteous legacy of their father. When God put Adam and Eve in the Garden, it was for them to establish His kingdom here on earth as it is in heaven. It was their opportunity to have a region to reign over, that is why we pray in this manner.

After we have the preliminaries of prayer established, you then begin to ask for the support you need to carry out the earthly assignment: "giving [of victory for] this day, your daily bread, [forgiveness] for our debts (sins), as we forgive [those that] sin against us: our debtors. You ask for [leadership] so you don't fall into temptation; you ask for deliverance (assistance) from [the] evil works that you know are here in the world (paraphrase of verses 11-13). Again, you declare your loving allegiance: "For thine is the kingdom, and the power, and the glory, forever. Amen."

This is considered the basic prayer model. As you grow in intimacy the dynamics of your prayer will change some. I mean you never go from calling your natural father and mother Dad and Mom to calling them by their first name, nor do you regard them dishonorably or disrespectfully. If you do then you should consider restoring the standard of respect and honor bestowed upon those who are in a seat of leadership and honor. However, as you physically grow up and mature, the context of your conversations do change. Here is a simple example that reflects this progression:

1. **Baby prayers:** You don't have any shame you just ask; relying upon God for every little thing! It's a stage of progress in prayer. Petitions, petitions, petitions, petitions. It's the "I need" stage.

2. **Adolescent prayers:** You have a slightly greater knowledge and understanding of some things, but you also still lack some. It moves into more specifics; the communication ability is expanded. It's more like "I need books and supplies for school."

3. **Adult prayers:** Mature, understands purpose of existence, purpose of prayer (intimacy), and the need for God's help to carry out your purpose (earthly assignment). You now move to become more of a conversationalist with Father God, and you are developing a deeper relationship with

Christ and His purposes as the "first of many brethren" (Lord, Leader, the Big Brother; example for earthly living with kingdom purpose) through prayer. The encouraging thing is that everybody goes through these same stages. Prayer is an awesome tool that is not only a line of communication, but a line of spiritual connection to our "home base" of heaven (Phil. 3:20; Heb. 11:13; 1Chron. 29:15; 1Pet. 2:11).

What is most important is that we never become satisfied with where we are, but that we continue to depths of intimacy that we have never known before until we are lost in love with God. Enoch walked with God until he was *not*; meaning he achieved a height and depth of intimacy where he was so hid in God he was translated (Gen. 5:21-24). I believe Enoch entered the place all believers should desire; a place where [we are *not*] people no longer see us but *only* see God through us. Prayer and constant intimacy afford this transformation.

CHAPTER 4

WORSHIPPER LIFE

How do you define worship? What comes to mind when you hear the term? Do you envision someone with arms lifted and kneeling before a physical monument or idol repeatedly bowing from knees to face? Do you see it as someone just singing praise and "worship" songs in a church service? However you imagine it there are likely some elements of truth, but there may be a mixture of some truth and some falsity, or maybe there's more to worship than you imagined. I'm a believer in the power of understanding, so let us first look up the definition of the word, open the scriptures, and pull it all together for a full picture on how to live as a true worshipper.

In the bible alone, you can read about not only people worshipping God (our Father, the God of Abraham, Isaac, and Jacob) but also being addressed on their worship of a

37

host of other gods. Worship is a practice that dates back to the beginning of time.

Worship is defined as:

☐ Reverent honor and homage paid to God or a sacred personage, or to *ANY* object regarded as sacred 2) formal or ceremonious rendering of such honor and homage (dictionary.com)

☐ To honor or show reverence for as a divine being or supernatural power 2) to regard with great or extravagant respect, honor, or devotion (Merriam-Webster.com)

☐ To kiss the hand to (towards) one, in token of reverence 2) among the Orientals, especially the Persians, to fall upon the knees and touch the ground with the forehead as an expression of profound reverence 3) in the NT by kneeling or prostration to do homage (to one) or make obeisance, whether in order to express respect or to make supplication (Strong-Lite)

☐ Meaning to kiss, like a dog licking his master's hand; to fawn [to court or favor by a flattering manner] or crouch to, that is, (literally or figuratively) prostrate oneself in homage (do reverence to, adore): worship (Strong's Definition)

The three consistent words we see within the definitions are reverence (deep respect), honor (great esteem), and homage (honor or respect shown publicly); the essence of worship is definitely captured by these.

David is known for his great display of worship for the Lord. In 1 Samuel 13:14 and Acts 13:22, the testimony is of David being "a man after [God's] own heart" and one who would fulfill His will; one who would pursue a life that would be pleasing to God; a worshipper life. There is a popular instance of this in 2Samuel 6:14-22 where David literally dances with great zeal, passion, and all his might in worship before the Lord. It was so "uncouth" that his wife, Michal, was embarrassed, and felt contempt towards him. Another scripture that connects this concept is Psalm 86:11 (AMP) which says, "Teach me Your way, O Lord, I will *walk and live* in Your truth; Direct my heart to fear Your name [with awe-inspired reverence and submissive wonder] (emphasis mine)." The goal in worship is giving all you have to please the one you are committed to love and serve. This prayer this cry of David's heart in Psalm 86 is one we should have as born-again believers when we envision and seek to be true worshippers. The desire to "walk and live" in worship, in awe-inspired reverence and submission (reverential fear).

Jesus commended the Samaritan woman at the well in John 4:23-24 in this way saying, "...the hour cometh, and now is when the true worshippers shall worship the Father in spirit and in truth: for the Father seeketh such to worship him." This "true" or unfeigned worship takes place inside, which is in the heart and spirit of the worshipper and is *visible* through a life lived transparently in righteous pursuit and honor towards the Lord. We honor and worship God when we show deference to his will, his established order, and systems; his worship preferences in our day to day lives. Therefore, we honor (worship) God in everything we do (1Cor. 10:31; Col. 3:17, 23; Prov. 3:6a).

This leads me to the point that worship *must* be pure (holy) and *desired* by the one being worshipped. Worship also must be specifically and appropriately directed, or we can so easily find ourselves worshipping other gods; utilizing their practices and behaving in ways that our God detests. Therefore, we must be very intentional about how we live. In both history and modern times, we see vile worship associated with idolatrous cults and gross misconduct that the Lord was explicit about us, his people, not being covenanted with or in any way defiled by (Deut.7:3-6). In the Old & New Testaments and in our modern day one prominent practice of worship is illicit sexual practices. The Canaanites practiced ritual prostitution and infant sacrifice under the guise of worship to the gods of Molech and Baal (Lev.18:6-30; 20:1-5). In fact, incest, homosexuality, bestiality, prostitution, fornication, pornography and even masturbation (all sexual acts that indulge the heart, spirit, and physical body), along with abortion (infanticide/termination of babies/pregnancies that are unwanted and not submitted to God's purposes) which is most often due to illegitimate sex practices and are all forms of worship, but *not* to the Lord our God (Lev. 18 – 19).

Paul also dealt with these plaguing practices in the church at Corinth (1Cor. 6:12-20; 10:14-22) and we certainly deal with them today whereby fornication (premarital sex) is almost as prominent and acceptable in the body of Christ as it is in the world. This is *NOT* acceptable and as born-again believers we must not do it or condone it; it is *not* acceptable worship to the Lord God. On the other hand, sexual intimacy between a husband and wife is honorable to God. Everything that *God* himself established is "good" and pleases him; it is when things are outside of the established order of God (inordinate) that it presents a problem. Remember, "true worship of God is essentially internal, a matter of the heart and spirit, [but] rooted in the *knowledge of* and *obedience to* the revealed Word of God (his will) [then displayed outwardly] (Orr, James.)." Though it is a heart matter, what is in our hearts is revealed in our words and deeds (Luke 6:45; Prov. 21:2; 24:12; 4:23; Ez. 11:21; 16:30). Therefore, our actions should align with what *God* wants if we are indeed offering worship to him.

Remember we, as born-again believers, have a covenant relationship with the Lord. He is not a mere idol or a figment of our imagination, but a living God. When we love someone, the goal is to show them honor and respect, to please them and of course make it known to all the world that they are in fact the love of our life. So, we respond passionately in their favor and "*LOVE* constrains (restricts) us" from treating them unfavorably, not laws or rules (2Cor. 5:14-15).

Now let us move on to some very acceptable ways in which we can and should worship God. We worship God as we:

- ☐ **Love him with our hearts**: (Mark 12:30; Matt. 22:37; Heb. 10:22; Luke 6:45; Eze. 36:26)

- ☐ **Love him through our actions**: (1John 3:18; Matt. 5:16; James 1:22; 3:13)

- ☐ **Love ourselves (his creation)**: (Mark 12:31; Eph. 5:29; Ps. 139:14; Prov. 19:8

- ☐ **Love others/neighbor (his creation)**: (Mark 12:31; Matt. 22:39; Phil. 2:3; Lev. 19:18; Luke 6:27; John 13:34-35; Rom. 13:8-10; Heb. 13:16

- ☐ **Pray (communicate frequently)**: (Ps. 4:1; 32:6; 66:19; 69:13; 141:2; Prov. 15:29; Mark 11:24; 1Thess. 5:17; Rom. 12:12; Phil. 4:5-7; Col. 4:2; James 5:13, 16; Rev. 8:3-4)

- ☐ **Study and meditate**: (on His word/precepts) (Jos. 1:8; Isa. 26:3; Ps. 1:2; 119:15, 48, 78, 97-99, 113, 148, 163; Ps. 19:7-11; 104:34; Prov. 4:20-22

- ☐ **Rest in quiet listening and stillness**: (John

16:13; Ps. 46:10; Hab. 2:20; 1Kings. 19:12; Ps. 131:2; 4:4; Ex. 14:14; Is. 30:15)

□ **Praise and give thanks**: (Ps. 100:4; 7:17; 107:1; 146:1-2; 50:23; Eph. 5:20; 1Thess. 5:18; Heb. 13:15)

□ **Sing songs of adoration**: (Col. 3:16; Psalm 96:1; 89:1; 100:2; 104:33; 2Chron. 20:22; Is. 42:10; Acts 16:25; 1Cor. 14:15; Eph. 5:19)

□ **Clap our hands and shout**: (Ps. 47:1; 132:9; 98:4; 2Chr. 15:14)

□ **Lift our hands**: (1Tim. 2:8; Ps. 134:2; 63:4; 119:48; 28:2; 141:2; Lam. 2:19; Neh. 8:6; Ezra 9:5)

□ **Kneel down and bow down**: (Neh. 8:6; Eph. 3:14; 2Kings 17:36; Ps. 5:7; 138:2; Zep: 2:11)

□ **Dance before him**: (Ps. 149:3; 30:11; 150:4; 2Sam. 6:14; 1Chr. 16:29; Ex. 15:20)

□ **Use instruments to glorify him**: (Ps. 150; 98:5-6; 81:2-3; 43:4; 149:3; 33:2; 71:22; 108:2; 144:9; 2Chr. 15:14)

□ **Give (time, talents, resources)**: (1Chr. 29:9;

2Cor. 9:7; Acts 20:35; Deut. 16:17; Mark 10:45; Luke 6:38; Mal. 3:10; Prov. 11:24; 28:27; 3:9; Luke 12:33-34; Ps. 96:8)

☐ **Keep his commandments**: (Deut. 6:1-2, 17; 8:1, 6; 11:1, 8, 32; 1King 2:3; 3:14; 8:61; 11:38; Ps. 78:7; Matt. 19:17-19; Ecc. 12:13; 1Cor. 7:19;1Tim. 6:14; 1John 3:22; 5:3; James 1:22)

☐ **Obey (are obedient to his instructions)**: (James 1:22; Luke 11:28; John 14:23; Prov. 6:20; 10:17; Deut. 28:1; 5:33; Rom. 12:2; 8:14; 1Kings 2:3; Jos. 1:8; Luke 9:23; Acts5:32)

☐ **Join in holy matrimony**: (Heb. 13:4; Gen. 2:24; 1:27-28; Mark 10:9; Matt. 19:6; Eph. 5:25-33; Ecc.4:9-12)

☐ **Live in holy singleness**: (1Cor. 7:32-34; Prov. 31:30; Rom. 12:1; Acts. 21:9; 1Cor. 7:7-8; Titus 2:6; Matt. 19:11-12)

☐ **Procreate (naturally and spiritually)**: (Gen. 1:28; 9:1, 7: 35:11; 28:3; Ps.127:3; 128:3; 115:14; Prov. 11:30; Dan. 12:3; 1Cor. 9:19-22; James 5:20; Jude 1:22-23)

☐ **Multiply (bring a return on his investmentsin us: gifts, talents, resources)**: (Gen 1:28; 12;2; 2Tim. 2:2; Acts 9:31; 12:24; Matt. 25:14-30; Prov. 21:5, 20; 13:22; 11:30; 31:16; 19:17; Ecc. 11:1-2; Is. 48:17; Jer. 29:7; Luke 19:13-26; Num. 27:20; Ex. 18:25; 1 Cor. 9:11)

☐ **Confess sin and repent**: (Ps. 51; 2Chron. 7:14; 1John 1:9; Acts 3:19; 2:38; Prov. 28:13; 1:23; Matt. 3:8; 2Chron. 30:9; 2Pet. 3:9; James 4:8; Rev. 3:19; Joel 2:13; Eze. 18:32; Mark 1:15; Zech. 1:3; Luke 15:10)

☐ **Serve humanity**: (Eph. 2:10; Prov. 28:27; 11:25; 19:17; Heb. 6:10; 13:2-3; Gal. 5:13; 1Pet. 4:10; Matt. 20:27-28; 23:11; 25:35-40; Rom. 12:13; Luke 6:35, 38; Gal. 6:10; Acts 20:35; Eph. 2:10; Col. 3:23-24; Is. 58:10; 2Cor. 9:7-9; Titus 3:8; 1Thess. 5:15; Phil. 2:3-4; 1John 3:17- 18)

☐ **Attend to widows and fatherless**: (James 1:27; Deut. 14:28-29; 24:19; 27:19; Is. 1:17; Ex. 22:22; 1Tim. 5:3; Ps. 82:3-4; 10:14; Prov. 19:17; Jer. 22:16; Zech. 7:9-10; Matt. 25:35-40)

☐ **Remember his marvelous works (all he's done and created)**: (1Chron 16:12, 24; Ps. 9:1; 96:2-4; 98:1; 105:1-2, 5; 139:14; 143:5; 77:10-12; Job37:14)

☐ **Seek his face**: (1Chron 16:10-11; Ps. 9:10; 105:3-4; 27::8; 34:10; 63:1 105:4; 119:2; Is.☐55:6; Jer. 29:13; Amos 5:4; Heb. 11:6; James 4:8)

"In other words, worship is the consummation of joy, [and our] chief end is to glorify God and to *enjoy* him forever (Gumbel)." "Dr. McGee says it this way, "worship is and forever will be us reflecting back to God what we think He's worth (McGee 2017)." I love God and I seek to be ever conscious of his presence and to worship him, love and honor him, all throughout my day, every day. It is not a chore but a joy to be in such a loving fulfilling relationship with my Lord Jesus and heavenly Father, and with the awesome Holy Spirit. May we all live the worshipper life!

CHAPTER 5

FORTIFYING THROUGH BIBLE STUDY

Similar to prayer, studying the Bible can be very intimidating for people when they lack the full understanding of how to do it, it's purpose, and how transformative it can really be. Bible study is not just for the scholarly. Bible study is the other bridge that moves us from distant stranger to intimacy with God. Remember, God made mankind in his likeness and image and desired familial relationship; to have heirs reigning in the region of the heavens called Earth (Gen. 26-28).

The Bible is made up of two main parts: The Old Testament and The New Testament. According to dictionary.com a testament is, "Law (a system of rules that a country recognizes as regulating the actions of its members and may enforce by the imposition of penalties; a statement of fact…); *a will*, especially one that relates to the disposition of one's personal property; either of the major portions of the Bible: the Mosaic or old covenant or dispensation or the Christian or new covenant or disposition; *a covenant*, especially between God and humans." Unmistakably, the Bible is an essential tool when learning about who God is, what God wants, what He does not want, what he has done, why he does what he does, and what our inheritance is as heirs. It should be the highest authority, the governing force of the born-again believer's life (Deut. 4:2, 8:3). In intimate prayer, God can and will often speak to you his will, but in studying the Bible you can read and learn of his will as it was written by men he spoke to (he inspired to write).

The Bible is broken into sections. There are the two main separations that we previously spoke of: The Old Testament (39 books) and The New Testament (27 books) which includes a total of sixty- six books. These books are categorically broken down into many sections.

The Old Testament has five sections.

1. The first section is called the Pentateuch, the "Five Books of Moses," or the Law which includes Genesis (1), Exodus (2), Leviticus (3), Numbers (4), and Deuteronomy (5).

2. The second section is the "history" books

(Joshua, Judges, Ruth, 1&2 Samuel, 1&2 Kings, 1&2 Chronicles, Ezra, Nehemiah, and Esther).

3. The third section of the Old Testament consists of the "poetry and wisdom books" (Job, Psalms, Proverbs, Ecclesiastes, and Song of Solomon).

4. Next is the fourth section which is called "the major prophets" (Isaiah, Jeremiah, Lamentations, Ezekiel, Daniel).

5. The last and fifth section of the Old Testament is "the minor prophets" (Hosea, Joel, Amos, Obadiah, Jonah, Micah, Nahum, Habakkuk, Zephaniah, Haggai, Zechariah, and Malachi).

The New Testament's twenty-seven books are also broken categorically into sections. The two main sections are the Gospels and the Letters (also known as Epistles) which are the Apostles responses to particular circumstances either of the writer or of one of the churches for encouragement, admonishment or just regarding Christian belief and how to live it out. These two sections can also be broken into five smaller categories.

1. The first section is called the Gospels (Matthew,

Mark, Luke, & John) which tells the story of Jesus Christ's life and his teachings. The books are essentially the same accounts/stories presented by different men.

2. The second section gives the account of the works of the Apostles (Acts).

3. The third section is called the Pauline Epistles which are books said to be written by the Apostle Paul (Romans, 1&2 Corinthians, Galatians, Ephesians, Philippians, Colossians, 1&2 Thessalonians, 1&2 Timothy, Titus, Philemon, and Hebrews - 14 books).

4. The fourth section is made up of the general epistles (James, 1&2 Peter, 1, 2, & 3 John, and Jude - 7 books).

5. The last and fifth section of the New Testament is written by the Apostle John (Revelation).

Many people are not really sure how to read the Bible. Do you read it from the beginning to the end like any other book? Or do you just read certain sections? The age-old question of new believers is, "Where do I start reading?"

That is a great question and has been answered differently depending on who has responded. However, most Christian leaders would recommend that it's best to begin reading in the Gospels (Matthew, Mark, Luke, and John) learning about Jesus and what he taught, which is the basis of our New Testament born-again Christian lifestyle.

The Old Testament is important as it "foreshadows" what was to come. Christ "came" in the flesh and bore the "content [state of satisfaction]" of the Old Testament. The New Testament is the revised will or New Covenant, which is the one that is "in effect" or "active" presently. It is what we need to know and understand in order to live like Jesus, as powerful spiritual kings, and sons of the Most High God. Remember Jesus Christ represents a "revised" order or the "new creature" lineage, "the first-born of many brethren (Rom. 8:29)." Our born-again life is this state of being under the order of Christ: the brethren. The more you study the Bible, the more you will become intimately acquainted with the Father God and the Lord Jesus Christ and your part as "heirs of God; joint-heirs with Christ (Rom. 8:17)."

In 2Timothy 2:15 (AMP) we are admonished to "study and do your best to present yourself to God approved, a workman [tested by trial] who has no reason to be ashamed; accurately handling and skillfully teaching the word of truth." In other words, read and study the Bible so that we can show God that we are actually His children because we live like Jesus Christ and our lives can be examined by others to learn from and see that mirroring of Christ's life in ours. Building a strong life as a born-again believer comes through much study and application of the Bible: doing it (James 1:22).

Some people may wonder why it is so emphasized, reading and studying this book, the Bible. I want to take you to a few other scriptures to show you why it is so important and how truly transformative it can be. In Romans 12:2 (AMP) we are told, "do *not* be conformed to this world [any longer with its superficial values and customs], but be transformed and progressively changed [as you mature spiritually] by the renewing of your mind [focusing on godly values and ethical attitudes], so that you may prove [for yourselves] what the will of God is; that which is good and acceptable and perfect [in His plan and purpose for you]." Here we see that studying the Bible transforms us by "renewing" or changing our minds, the way we think and govern our lives; from a worldly carnal [fleshly] thought pattern to a godly heavenly [spiritual] way of thinking. This is the greatest transformation one can experience moving from a weak natural human being to become a strong super-natural spiritual being. It is similar to the transformation that happens with those who enter any armed military branch where they go in a simple civilian and come out a trained refined soldier.

In Hebrews 4:12 (AMP) it says, "For the word of God [the Bible] is living and active and full of power [making it operative, energizing, and effective]. It is sharper than any two-edged sword, penetrating as far as the division of the soul and spirit [the completeness of a person], and of both joints and marrow [the deepest parts of our nature], exposing and judging the very thoughts and intentions of the heart." This scripture unfolds to us how powerful the word of God is in its ability to transform us. Some people go through "plastic surgery" to physically alter their appearance. Studying the Bible performs like a "spiritual surgery" that cuts away and changes all the mindsets, habits, behaviors, etc. that are contrary to a godly and supernatural kingdom lifestyle.

In 1Peter 2:2 we are admonished to "...crave [long for]

the pure milk of the word, so that by it you may be nurtured and grow in respect to salvation [your born-again/transformed life] ..." This particular scripture is reiterating to us how important the word is to our growth, by relating it to babies needing milk to grow. Born-again believers need the "milk of the word" in order to grow spiritually strong.

I want to draw your attention to my intentional use of the word "study" rather than "read" in my address on how we are to engage with the Bible. Reading can add head knowledge and is casual, but studying is an aggressive consumption of the material with the purpose of transformation and execution; it embeds it in our hearts. Studying is not passive nor is it empty of results. Matthew 7:24-25 (KJV) says, "Therefore whosoever heareth these sayings of mine, AND doeth them, I will liken him unto a wise man, which built his house upon a rock: and the rain descended, and the floods came, and the winds blew, and beat upon that house; and it fell not: for it was founded upon a rock." Studying the word of God *and* doing it solidifies you in your reborn spirit and in the Truth [Jesus Christ who redeemed you]. One who studies proves himself to be a true disciple.

PART THREE:

MATURING: FOUNDATIONAL DISCIPLESHIP II

CHAPTER 6

UNDERSTANDING THE HOLY SPIRIT'S ROLE

T here is so much to be said in this chapter of understanding the Holy Spirit and his role. Many people are not only confused about his role but are even fearful of him. He is referred to by several different names or titles throughout the scripture which differ depending on the nature or function of his ministry being carried out. Some of the names/titles are used interchangeably depending upon the translation you are reading (i.e., King James, Amplified, NIV, etc.). Some of the most common ones are:

☐ **Spirit of God** (Gen. 1:2, Matt. 3:16, 1Cor. 2:11)

☐ **Spirit of the Lord** / **Spirit** (Judges 3:10, 2Cor. 3:17, Acts 11:12, Rom. 8:16; Eph. 3:16)

☐ **Holy Spirit** / **Holy Ghost** (Mt. 12:32; Acts 2:4,

33; 4:31; 2Pet. 1:21; 1Cor. 2:13; Acts 9:31; 1John 5:7)

☐ **Comforter / Helper/ Counselor/ Advocate** (John 14:16,26; 15:26, 16:7; Acts 9:31)

☐ **Spirit of Wisdom**(Is. 11:2)

☐ **Spirit of Truth / Revealer** (John 14:17, 16:13-14)

☐ **Convicter of sin** (John 16:7-11)

☐ **Seal, Deposit, or Earnest** (2Cor. 1:22, 5:5; Eph.1:13-14)

☐ **Intercessor**(Rom. 8:26)

☐ **Guide** (John 16:13)

☐ **Author of Scripture** (2Tim. 3:16)

☐ **Teacher** (1Cor. 2:13; John 14:26)

☐ **Witness** (Rom. 8:16, Heb. 2:4, 10:15; 1John 5:6).

I believe the terms spirit or ghost often evoke feelings of fear due to insufficient knowledge along with the perverted media usage of components of the spirit realm. Most people experience reluctance and/or reservations and caution when they are unfamiliar with something and this is the case with their lack of understanding about the Holy Spirit. Many do not realize that *he* is such a "gentleman": loving strong and serving in nature. I want to put emphasis on him being a "person" of the godhead and in that way has feelings and should be treated with regard as such. Ephesians 4:30 tells us he can be "grieved" and 1Thessaloinians 5:19 tells us he can be "quenched" in terms of the exercise of his will, and in Acts 7:51 we see he can be resisted. Therefore, regard him with honor as you would the Father and the Lord Jesus, and keep these things in mind as I continue to share about his personhood and his character traits and responsibilities to usward.

In the Greek, the word used to represent him is "parakletos" from which we get "paraclete" which means "called to one's side." According to His role "at our side" it is as a comforter and partner, an advocate or intercessor, a helper, counselor, and teacher. "[He aids us in seeing] the things of Christ, teaching us of things to come (all things), quickening our memories for past teachings, bearing witness to Christ, dwelling in believers, enabling us to do greater works than those of Christ, as well as convicting us of sin in our lives of righteousness and of judgment (Orr, J.)"

In Genesis 1:2 is where we first see the Holy Spirit at work "moving upon the face of the waters." Throughout scripture we see him "doing" works on behalf of the godhead. He is the executor of the covenant; the person appointed by a testator to carry out the terms of their will (lexico.com). He was sent to lead, guide, and teach us how to understand what we have been given access to from the heavenlies and how to execute the kingdom of heaven in the earth as well (1Cor. 2:12). Let us take a look at some of these things in the scriptures:

> ☐ "Do you not know that your body is a ***temple of the Holy Spirit*** who is within you, whom you have [received as a gift] from God, and that you are not your own [property]? You were bought with a price [you were actually purchased with the precious blood of Jesus and made His own]. So then, honor and glorify God with your body. (1Cor. 6:19-20 AMP)"

In 1Corinthians 6:19-20 we see that *we* are homes / temples for the Holy Spirit in the earth. We received him from God and are to glorify God in our bodies by and through him. It is an immensely powerful concept and understanding that God would put such a power source inside of us to aid us in living out this born-again Christian walk, as victors. Having the Holy Spirit inside of us makes it both untrue and insulting to God when we say we cannot do things. God can do *all* things. So, with Him *we* can do *all* things as well (Phil 4:13). This, like every concept connected with our salvation, requires faith and submission to walk in, to display. Let us look at another key scripture targeting his role.

☐ "But the Comforter, which is the Holy Ghost, whom the Father will send in my name, he shall **teach you all things**, and **bring all things to your remembrance**, whatsoever I have said unto you. (John 14:26 KJV)"

Recognizing and submitting to the Holy Spirit as teacher is another really big component of the relationship we are to have with him. In the natural, someone can be a teacher, but if you do not show up to their class and/or submit yourself to their instruction, you will not learn that subject and you will not have success in that program of study. Well, likewise, if we do not yield to and submit to the

Holy Spirit's leadership and instruction, we shortchange our experience and we lack measures of knowledge and wisdom that we could have. In addition, he helps us to remember the teachings of Christ which is vital for this earthly journey. Christ is our greatest example of how to live in the earth while representing and accomplishing the mandates of heaven. Please realize that the Holy Spirit is a gift. Once a gift is given it is up to the recipient to use the gift or not. In Luke, we see that not only is the Holy Spirit a gift, but the Father does not force him on us; we must in fact ask for this gift.

☐ "If you, then, being evil [that is sinful by nature], know how to give good gifts to your children, how much more will your heavenly Father **give the Holy Spirit to those who ask** and continue to ask Him! (Luke 11:13 AMP)"

There are several other scriptures that I recommend that you search out as they support this principle that repenting, praying, obedience and just straight out asking for the Holy Spirit will move the Father to dispense him to you.

☐ Acts 5:32 – given based on obedience

☐ Acts 4:31 – given through prayer

☐ Acts 19:5-6 – given by laying on of hands/prayer

☐ Acts 2:38 – given based on repentance/prayer

Again, the Holy Spirit is a gift and gifts are blessings, meaning they add value to us. The Holy Spirit doesn't only live in us, teach us, comfort us, help us in our weaknesses, bring back to our remembrance the things Christ has said, but he also comes bearing a host of other gifts. He is literally "the gift that keeps on giving" and I really want us to come to fully understand the value of and power of the Holy Spirit working in our lives. Knowing more intimately who He is and understanding his role, along with building a solid relationship with him in yielded trust will prepare us to operate in his gifts more readily.

CHAPTER 7

GIFTS OF THE HOLY SPIRIT

Heretofore, we have learned about our role as born- again believers, we learned about faith, prayer, and building a solid foundation through the study of the word. At this point, we have also gotten a good sense of the Holy Spirit's role and looked at many scriptures to evidence that as well. Now, let us look at the many gifts that He brings and makes available to the born-again Christian believer to walk in victory and dominion in the earth.

In Acts 1:8 we learn that the Holy Spirit enables us to have power and we see in Galatians 5:22-23 that we gain fruits and outgrowths from the Spirit that are to be observable in our lives with him. These "fruits" are elements of the "divine nature;" the character of God added to us to build our character and make us rise above our "fleshly" natural old selves into our "supernatural" born-again, new selves. Here are the fruits of the spirit as defined in combination by Strong-Lite, Strong's, Dictionary.com, along with some personal explanation and exemplifying scriptures:

1. **Love** – brotherly love, good will, benevolence; agape a.k.a. the God kind of love (benevolent one). It is rooted in a decision to extend care, compassion, and beneficial actions towards another. Love is not based on how one feels but on a conscious decision to operate like God; righteously. We choose to love."For God so loved the world that he [*DECIDED* and] gave his only begotten Son, that whosoever believeth in him should not perish, but have everlasting life (John 3:16 KJV emphasis mine)." Love is an extraordinarily powerful seat and when we operate from it we "fulfill [achieve] the entirety of God's law/commands" and become a premier conduit for the power of God to flow through.

2. **Joy** – gladness, cheerfulness, and calm delight. True joy manifests based on a constancy of gratitude for God's love, all He is and all He has

given us. "...in your presence [*and in every thought of you*] is fullness of joy (Psalm 16:11b AMP emphasis mine)."

3. **Peace** – a state of tranquility; restful safety and security. Peace manifests through faith/trust in God, and in his ability to maintain sovereign control. "You will keep in perfect and constant peace the one whose mind is steadfast [that is, committed and focused on You – in both inclination and character], Because he trusts and takes refuge in You [with hope and confident expectation] (Isaiah 26:3 AMP)."

4. **Longsuffering/Forbearance** – Bearing the burden of responsibility through extensive patience, endurance, and constancy. It manifests in patient restraint from swift wrath and judgement. "[He] is longsuffering us-ward, not willing that any should perish, but that all should come to repentance (2Peter 3:9c KJV)."

5. **Gentleness/Kindness** – mild, pleasant, benevolent, and gracious: benignity. A byproduct of love. "So, as God's own chosen people, who

are holy [set apart, sanctified for His purpose] and well-beloved [by God Himself], put on a heart of compassion, kindness, humility, gentleness, and patience [which has the power to endure whatever injustice or unpleasantness comes, with good temper] (Colossians 3:12)."

6. **Goodness** – high moral standards, virtue, beneficence, of perfect nature, useful; excellency, power, perfectness (on a heavenly standard; nothing missing or out of divine order). It is a manifestation of God's heart and is expressed through his creation. "And God saw everything that he had made, and behold, it was very good (Genesis 1:31 KJV)."

7. **Faith** – assurance; conviction of truth, belief that God exists and is the creator and ruler of all things; fidelity, reliability. Based on revelation of Hebrews 11, it is a substance of an unseen currency that viably plays as a medium of exchange for things from the spirit realm to be manifested in the earthen realm. "Now faith is the substance of things hoped for, the evidence

of things not seen (Hebrews 11:1)."

8. **Meekness/Humility** – gentleness, mildness; by implication humility; submissiveness; patience *without* resentment. I have heard it called "strength under control" and we know that God himself gives grace, empowerment, to the humble so it's a powerful position. "Behold, I send you forth as sheep in the midst of wolves; be ye therefore wise as serpents, and harmless as doves (Matt 10:16)." (Strong's Definition & Merriam-Webster)

9. **Temperance/Self-control** – self-control, the virtue of one who masters his desires and passions; emotional restraint; moderation in action, thought, or feeling. Manifests in vigilance and sobriety to holy Christ centered living and consciousness as to not be overtaken by the adversary. "Be sober, be vigilant; because your adversary the devil, as a roaring lion, walketh about, seeking whom he may devour: (1Peter 5:8)."

In Acts 4:31, we see them speaking the word of God

with boldness on account of the Holy Spirit. In Romans 8:12-14 we see, "if we live [have our lives governed] by the Spirit [releasing ourselves to his leadership] we [can] put to death [halt] [all] the [worldly, inordinate, sinful] deeds of the body and live [prosper in a secured seat in the family of God as sons] (paraphrased)." Hallelujah!! Praise God for all these wonderful attributes and abilities we are able to access by having the Holy Spirit working in and through us. The Holy Spirit aids us tremendously in living a godly kingdom lifestyle.

I now want to look at another set of extraordinary gifts or "diversities of gifts" that come with the Holy Spirit; it's the "gifts of the spirit" according to 1Corinthians 12:1 – 11 and Romans 12:6-8. These gifts are given for us saints (born-again believers), the body of Christ, to profit/benefit from them. I will expound on the core list of 9 from 1Corinthians 12 here, including a basic understanding of their operation and list scriptural example(s) of its manifestation in history:

1. **Word of wisdom**: an ability to access and speak or have godly insight and exceptional strategies from the heavenly realm **(Joseph to Pharaoh Gen. 41:33-40)**

72

2. **Word of knowledge**: an ability to access and speak or know things that exceeds one's natural educational and experiential knowledge; supernatural intel **(Jesus to the Samaritan women in John 4:15-19; Ananias to Paul in Acts 9:10-17)**

3. **Gift of prophecy**: an ability to prophesy (see, hear, and say) something from the spirit realm; most often it is life bearing (edifying, exhorting, and comforting). It may have futuristic elements but not necessarily. Let me clarify that the ability to prophesy does *NOT* indicate one is a prophet (officer) as listed in Ephesians 4:11. Remember, we are speaking about abilities that are made available based on the Holy Spirit coming upon them. Here is an example of God literally using **a donkey to speak upon seeing an angel in Numbers 22:30-33**, and **Saul and his messengers prophesy in 1Samuel 19:20-24** under the "gift of prophecy". So, we know that the ability to prophesy alone does not make one a prophet. There are many other attributes and most specifically a significant designation of

authority given to an actual prophet (officer). However, every believer can prophecy by the Holy Spirit's gifting.

4. **Gift of faith**: an ability to believe in an exceptional way that supernaturally produces; it encourages those observing and spurs them on to believe in a greater way **(Moses with the children of Israel in Exodus 14:13-16)**

5. **Gifts of healings**: an ability to minister various kinds of healings to the sick in a supernatural measure **(Elisha with Naaman in 2Kings 5:9-14; Peter heals lame man Acts 3:1-9)**

6. **Working of miracles**: an ability to do exceptional or "miraculous" acts which defy or surpass scientific, natural, and universal ideologies knowledge and laws **(Paul's very body healing those not present Act 19:11- 12)**

7. **The discerning of spirits**: a shrewd or heightened ability to judge, determine, and distinguish the motivation or spirit in operation in a statement made, situation, or visibly operating within a person **(Jesus discerning no**

deceit/guile in Nathanael John 1:47; Peter with Simon the sorcerer Acts 8:18-23)

8. **Different kinds of tongues**: an ability to situationally manifest different languages (including heavenly tongues) that is not one's native language nor is it one they have learned through schooling or study **(Jewish men from all nations Acts 2:4, 6-11; any/all Christians who are filled with the evidence of speaking in other tongues 1Cor 14:2, 22)**

9. **Interpretation of tongues**: an ability to hear and gain understanding (interpretation) of a language that one has not learned (including and most often specifically interpretation of the heavenly tongues) **(any/all Christian believers 1Cor. 14:13- 14, 27-28)**

God, through the Holy Spirit, can manifest any of these gifts to any believer at any time to profit; for his kingdom purposes and the strengthening and establishing of the body of Christ according to Romans 1:11. Hopefully, this chapter has given you a clearer sense of these capabilities that you can walk in as one yielded to the Spirit of the living God.

Additionally, may you understand more certainly how vital and instrumental the Holy Spirit is in the life of a born-again Christian believer.

CHAPTER 8

UNDERSTANDING KINGDOM RULE

There is an interesting thing about the times we live in and it's that you more readily hear "Christians" using popular clichés such as "we're a kingdom minded church" or "we keep it kingdom." There is in fact more chatter about kingdom, but most people cannot give a viable explanation of the kingdom of God nor are they actuating it in their lives. The kingdom of God brings life, healings, liberty from strongholds and oppressions, and victory over all the works of darkness and its defeating attributes.

Then why are so many "kingdom minded" born- again believers *not* living victoriously *nor* aiding others in gaining victory? Well, true earthly victories are hinged upon our understanding of the kingdom of God. Remember, to those watching, Jesus did not have victory when he submitted to the process of capture, being beaten, scourged, and dying on a cross, but we know differently. Let's forge ahead and gain a greater understanding of what a kingdom is, how it operates structurally and what God's kingdom looks like in our lives as His elect.

First, we should know that the bible is written by a king for kings and kingdom constituents. I shared earlier in the book that kingdoms are either established by or seized by kings. There are also instances where a king or more likely a queen may be grafted into a royal lineage through the covenant of marriage. Being royalty is not a happenstance, but something that must be obtained lawfully and only by these few methods. In reiteration, kingship/ royalty can only be obtained by inheritance through lineage, through covenant (i.e., marriage), or by one forcefully taking possession of a kingdom as in seizing it from a king that is presently ruling by capture or by killing him.

One of the primary reasons that most people are not really acquainted with the structure and operations of a kingdom is because of the institution of democracy. In a democracy, all qualified citizens (the people) get to vote for its leading officials and there are systems in place to give the people a measure of input into who serves in that hierarchy. In the United States of America and some other countries there is voting for those serving at the federal level such as the President, those in Congress and the Senate, and for those in the state and local government (i.e., Governors, Mayors, and City Councilman, etc.). These societal norms, though they have their benefits, have in some ways inhibited our understanding of, and distanced us from the ways of God, and from the biblical example of kingdom rulership.

A kingdom, however, is a territory or area ruled by a king: a monarchical form of government. We see countless examples of this in the scriptures, reflecting both the heavenly kingdom and the earthly one. In a kingdom, there are still officials with governing authority (i.e., governors, judges, ambassadors, etc.) as well but there is one main difference. How they all got there. In a kingdom, those with delegated authority are chosen and appointed by a sovereign. In the kingdom of God, it's the Sovereign Lord. The Lord God himself, in his sovereignty, chooses and appoints kings, prophets and other governing officials throughout time. He has used angels, prophets, and apostles as his instruments to inaugurate leading men and women throughout history. We see this example in the choosing and anointing of Saul, Israel's first king in 1Samuel 9:15-10:27 by the *prophet* Samuel. We also see this enactment with the *angel* Gabriel declaring the Lord's appointment of the prophet's office upon John (the Baptist) in Luke 1:13-19 and over Mary as the carrier of our Lord Jesus Christ in Luke 1:26-38. It is clear as we see through scripture that the Sovereign Lord has always and continues to rule and reign from his heavenly throne invoking that rulership upon both heavenly beings and earthly vessels for his own purposes. True Sovereignty, Monarchy *not* democracy.

Let us look deeper at this concept of the bible being by a king, for kings and kingdom constituents, as assuredly we will detect an abundance of royal verbiage and kingdom purpose being fulfilled. In Luke 1:32-33(KJV) it reads, "He [Jesus] shall be great, and shall be called the **Son of the Highest**: and the **Lord** God shall **give unto him the throne of his father David**: and he shall **reign** over the house of Jacob forever; and of **his kingdom** there shall be no end." Now clearly, we can all see this is kingdom language here *and* kingdom purpose. We gain context now in understanding that Jesus was sent with a specific purpose, as a king to do what kings do: seize territories and rule and reign over them. Clearly his work was not for us to just have a "ticket to heaven" as some may think. Let us build on this and look at several more scriptures to sequentially get a broader picture of the Sovereign Lord's plans and purposes from the beginning being rolled out before us in his testimony, the bible.

CHAPTER 9

KING JESUS' JOURNEY ON EARTH

The loss of the kingdom...

Remember in Genesis 1, God made man and gave him "dominion [kingdom rule] over all the earth" and by Genesis 3, he [man] had lost the throne through deception and death by the serpent (Satan). "The noun Satan, Hebrew for adversary, occurs nine times in the Hebrew bible with five of the instances used to describe a human military, political or legal opponent and four times with reference to a divine being (biblicalarchaeology.org)." Serpent in the Strong's is "to hiss, that is, whisper a (magic) spell; generally, to prognosticate; enchant, divine. Herein we better understand the backdrop, that a strategy by an opponent was set against Adam to dethrone him "legally" or "militarily." Kingdom issues.

The plan for recovery...

It was through a divine strategy from the throne of heaven that Jesus would come into the earth, clothed in humanity, and be born of a woman through an earthly lineage of royalty (David's) to *"seek and save THAT which was lost [the kingdom and those embondaged constituents]"* and "legally" recoup it and them. (Luke 19:10; Matt 18:11; 1Tim. 3:16; Heb. 2:14; John 1:14; Phil. 2:6-7; Rom. 8:3; Matt.1;1; 15:22; John 7:42; Rom. 1:3; 2Tim 2:8). Isaiah speaks of the Lord's plan in chapter 11:1, "and there shall come forth a rod out of the stem of Jesse [King David's father] and a branch shall grow out of his roots: and the spirit of the Lord shall rest upon him, the spirit of wisdom and understanding, the spirit of counsel and might, the spirit of knowledge and of the fear of the Lord..." In Numbers 24:17 "[the Messiah] is seen, but not now; beholden but not near. A star to come out of Jacob; *a scepter [kingship]* will rise out of Israel (paraphrased)." Jeremiah also declares this in 23:5-6, "Behold, the days come, saith the Lord, that *I will raise* unto David *a righteous branch and a King shall reign* and prosper and shall *execute judgement and justice* in the earth. In his days, Judah shall be saved, and Israel shall dwell safely: and this is his name whereby he shall be called, THE LORD OUR RIGHTEOUSNESS." Just like Gabriel spoke Christ's existence to Mary, so the prophets spoke Christ's existence into time and space through prophecy in the Old Testament. You may look at these other instances in 2 Samuel 7:12-17, Micah 5:2 and Isaiah 7:14. Jesus Christ, our salvation and redeemer, was sent to regain what was lost by Adam in the garden; earthly dominion [our kingship], obedient sonship [being righteous heirs] and eternal life [experiencing no sting of death/eternal separation from God].

The process of time...

And like an extremely intense chess game, much time passed with many strategic moves being made to reclaim the kingdom. Christ makes his grand entrance, born in Bethlehem as prophesied and being recognized at birth *as king* by the wise men in Matthew 2:1-2; publicly announcing having seen "his star" and referring to him as *King of the Jews*. Mind you, this stirred the current reigning natural king, who instantly moved to protect his kingdom from seizure. King Herod, in that effort, takes counsel of "all the chief priests and scribes" and by "[slaying all the children that were in Bethlehem, two years old and under... (Matt 2:4-8, 16-17)." See, all this to protect his natural kingdom. What lengths has our God taken to ensure the retrieval of the kingdoms of the earth? He has gone to great lengths by using infinite wisdom and calculated moves.

The Lord continues to "actively watch over his word to fulfill it" based on Jeremiah 1:12 and continues to unfold the fullness of his plan using Joseph and Mary as guardians of the word of truth, both in physicality (as parents) and spiritually partnering with the word spoken to them by the angelic visitation (Luke 2:19). Essentially, Christ was hidden in plain sight.

Most of us can attest to knowing "gifted" children, who at young ages are actively displaying the connectedness they have with their life's purpose. Whether it's a child who is exceptional at singing, playing an instrument, in a sport or highly intellectual and exceptional at articulating their thoughts, we know that when God writes the purposes of man into his DNA, it often manifests at noticeably young ages. Although there is not much scripture written specifically about Jesus' youth, we do see him intrinsically connected to his purpose in the instance at the temple. In

Luke 2:41-52 we read that at the age of 12, he is not only drawn to the temple among the teachers but is casually sitting and engaging with them as if it's totally normal. Then his cynical response to his mother, "Why did you have to look for Me? Did you not know that I had to be in my Father's house?" His statement indicates that based on the nature of his birth and his life purpose, assuredly manifesting as he grew, that his behavior should not have surprised them, although it did (Luke 2:49-50 AMP). Even though we see a beautiful shift with the connected statements, "his mother kept all these sayings in her heart" and "Jesus increased in wisdom and stature and in favor with God and man (Luke 2:51d-52)."

It concludes to us at this point that not only is Mary done being "amazed" or "surprised" by her son's continued greatness showing up in everyday life situations, but now she is holding fast to these experiences as evidence of what she has always known: God has a great plan to be unfolded by this miraculous son. Jesus, after this temple incident is now exponentially growing in wisdom, and stature [age, maturity, and readiness] and in favor with God and man (Luke 2:52).

Be mindful to observe here that the power of death and enslavement to sin that blinds, was at work in every human from the time of Adam and Eve's offense in the garden (Ps. 51:5; 2Cor. 4:4; John 12:39-40; Eph. 2:3, 4:18; Gen 6:5, 2:17). So, despite Mary and Joseph's being chosen to parent Jesus, they were still subject to experiencing this "blindness [confusion or disbelief]" that manifests in *all* who are born in sin. They have a sense of things, based on the prophecy of his birth, but vacillate between accepting what they have been told is truth above the faculties of their very natural human experience. This plagues all humans and only upon becoming born-again can we masterfully overcome it by the help of the Holy Spirit. It is this insertion of death into the DNA that has corrupted and prevented man from fully being able to "know" God and be intimately acquainted with the divine nature [hereditary characteristics] *without* salvation and rebirth through Christ (2Pet 1:4; John 3:5-6; 2Cor 2:9-10; Col. 1:26-27).

Full disclosure...

Fast forward, Jesus Christ is at full maturity and ready to fulfill his purpose to legally redeem man and the kingdom reign lost in Eden. He is baptized by John, approved and commissioned openly by the Father and the Holy Spirit, then tested in the wilderness by the devil (Matt. 3:13-17; 4:1-11). He begins his public ministry and shows his ambassadorship by displaying the kingdom of heaven through many miracles, signs, and wonders (Acts 2:22).

All these acts were indications of attachment to deity [divine status]. As the elect, born-again believers redeemed by Christ; it enables us the same capabilities in our "divine nature" (2Pet. 1:4). According to Mark 16:17-18, "... these signs shall follow [accompany] *them that believe*; in my name [attachment to deity] shall they cast out devils; they shall speak with new tongues; they shall take up serpents; if they drink any deadly thing, it shall not hurt them; they shall lay hands on the sick and they shall recover." Throughout history, as well as in present times, *anyone* can do signs wonders and miracles if they use faith [spiritual currency] and tap into a spiritual source [a god/deity]: whether it's the devil, false gods or the one true and living God of Abraham, Isaac, Jacob (Acts 2:43; 5:12; Heb. 2:4).

Historically, people have either been awe struck by these works or fearful of them because of sheer ignorance. The worship and solicitation of supernatural powers other than

God has been around since the beginning. In my experience and observation of the way Christian believers respond to this is that most have not understood true worship, and the power that spiritual connection can afford. In addition, the only association or understanding of "worshipping" of gods that they have is linked negatively to pagan worship and therefore in their "modernized intellectuality" they actually shun true worship rather than just appropriately placing it upon the true Sovereign Lord God Almighty.

Familiar examples of opposing players using pagan gods and demonic sources were seen in the story with Moses contending with Pharaoh's "wise men, sorcerers: magicians of Egypt" which is found in Exodus 7:11, 22; 8:7. We see Elijah confronting the prophets of Baal in 1 Kings 18:20-40. We see Peter encountering sorcerers in his ministry (Acts 8:9- 24), then Paul dealt with this issue also (Acts 13:6- 12; 16:16-18; 19:8-20) and we even see John's revelation of "spirits of devils doing miracles" in Rev 16:14.

Therefore, you must remember that signs, wonders, and miracles are *not* exclusive to born-again believers, but are a sign that the one performing them *does* have "faith/belief" and worshipful attachment to some form of deity. The Holy Spirit enables us born-again believers the ability to discern the source. If we rise in our understanding of what we have gained in our redemption, rise in our faith/belief in God and the *reality* of who He is and His power [superiority above all other gods]; rise to worship and full submission for His manifestation in and through us, *WE* will bring His kingdom to every sphere we touch just like Jesus and all those in the scriptures.

As Jesus is matured and began operating in ministry publicly, he candidly speaks of his identity and purpose. They are as follows:

☐ ***As our salvation***: In Luke 19:9-10 Jesus says to Zacchaeus, "this day is ***salvation*** [redemption; liberty] come to this house, forasmuch as ***he*** also is a son of Abraham [God's promised offspring; represents manifestation of faith and obedience]. For the Son of man is ***come to seek and to save that which was lost*** (Gen 22:18)."

☐ ***As the way, the truth, and the life***: In John 14:6, "Jesus says, ***I am the way, the truth, and the life: no man cometh unto the Father, but by me.***" He is also letting us know clearly, he is the one

91

designated and sent to restore our position of intimacy with the Father that was lost when Adam and Eve were put at a distance and "drove out of the garden" (Gen. 3:23-24). He is the source of all truth and knowledge about Father God and the *only* way to get to him.

☐ *As the door [entrance/portal] for kingdom access*: In John 10:9 Jesus says, "*I am the door*: by me if any man enter in, he shall be saved, and shall go in and out, and find pasture [not wanting for the needful supplies for true life] (John 10:7, 9)." He is the passageway.

☐ *As the light of the world*: In John 8:12 Jesus says, "*I am the light of the world*: he that followeth me shall not walk in darkness, but shall have the light of life." Christ enables us to walk through a dark and lost world clearly with illumination, both naturally and spiritually to maneuver through this life in victory.

☐ *As the bread of life*: In John 6:35 Jesus says, "*I am the bread of life*: he that cometh to me shall never hunger; and he that believeth on me shall never thirst (John 6:35, 41, 48, 51)." He sustains us both spiritually and naturally.

☐ *As the good shepherd*: In John 10:11 Jesus says, "*I am the good shepherd*: the good shepherd giveth his life for the sheep (John 10:11, 14)." He declares his commitment to fully care for us both naturally and spiritually by his death.

☐ *As the resurrection and the life*: In John 11:25 Jesus says, "*I am the resurrection and the life*: he that believeth in me, though he were dead, yet shall he live." He assures us of both spiritual life in him here, when we are born-again, and after physical death having life eternal in glory.

☐ *As the true vine*: In John 15:1 Jesus says, *I am the true vine*, and my Father is the husbandman (John 15:1, 5)." He affirms that he is the source that will connect us to the fullness of life and "fruit bearing" abilities rooted in the Father.

☐ *As Alpha and Omega*: In Revelation 1:8 Jesus says, "*I am Alpha and Omega*, the beginning and the ending...which is, and was, and is to come, the Almighty." He allows us to know the nature of his infinity which has no end: boundlessness.

Christ came as the manifestation of those things we just read, but he also came with multiple purposes to be accomplished as well. Here are the purposes below:

- ☐ **To reign as king**. In Isaiah 9:6-7 (AMP) it says, "For to us a Child shall be born, to us a Son shall be given; the government [empire/ kingdom] shall be upon His shoulder, and His name shall be called Wonderful Counselor, Mighty God, Everlasting Father, Prince of Peace. There shall be no end to the increase of His government [empire/ kingdom] and of peace, [He shall rule] on the throne of David and over his kingdom, To establish it and uphold it with justice and righteousness; from that time forward and forevermore [an eternal kingdom]. The zeal of the Lord of hosts will accomplish this."

- ☐ **To establish a new lineage of kings (obedient sons)**. Christ became the firstborn; the establishment of a lineage "[with us being]

94

conformed to the image of [Christ], that he might be the firstborn among many brethren [heirs]" (Rom. 8:29).

- ☐ **To make us partakers of the divine nature**. In 2 Peter 1:4 it says, "Whereby are given unto us exceeding great and precious promises: that by these ye might be partakers [sharers] of the divine nature, having escaped the corruption that is in the world through lust."

- ☐ **To restore dominion to us in the new linage**. In Luke 22:29 it reads, "And I appoint unto *you* a kingdom, as my Father hath appointed unto me; that ye may eat and drink at my table in my kingdom and sit on thrones judging the twelve tribes of Israel."

- ☐ **To give us abundant life**. In John 10:10 it says, "The thief cometh not, but for to steal and to kill, and to destroy; I am come that they might have life and that they might have it more abundantly."

- ☐ **To demonstrate true humility, obedience, and submission**. In Philippians 2:5-8 (AMP) it says,

"Have this same attitude in yourselves which was in Christ Jesus [look to Him as your example in selfless humility], who although He existed in the form and unchanging essence of God [as One with Him, possessing the fullness of all the divine attributes – the entire nature of deity] did not regard equality with God; a thing to be grasped or asserted [as if He did not already possess it or was afraid of losing it], but emptied Himself [without renouncing or diminishing His deity, but only temporarily giving up the outward expression of divine equality and His rightful dignity] by assuming the form of a bondservant and being made in the likeness of men [He became completely human but was without sin, being fully God and fully man.] After He was found [in terms of His] outward appearance as a man [for a divinely appointed time], He humbled Himself [still further] by becoming obedient [to the Father] to the point of death, even death on a cross."

☐ **To be the second and greater Adam**. In

Romans 5:14-15 (AMP) it says, "Yet death ruled [over mankind] from Adam to Moses [the lawgiver], even over those who had not sinned as Adam did. Adam is a type of Him (Christ) who was to come [but in reverse – Adam brought destruction; Christ brought salvation]. But the free gift [of God] is not like the trespass [because the gift of grace overwhelms the fall of man]. For if many died by one man's trespass [Adam's sin], much more [abundantly] did God's grace and the gift [that comes] by the grace of the one Man, Jesus Christ, an overflow to [benefit] the many."

☐ **To destroy the power of death and bondage, while in human flesh, that it <u>may rightfully be accessible to us "his brethren", the redeemed</u>**. In Hebrews 2:14-17 it says, "Forasmuch then as the children are partakers of flesh and blood, he [Jesus] also himself likewise took part of the same [humanity; as flesh and blood]; that through death he might destroy him that had the power of death, that is

97

the devil; And deliver them [us] who through fear of death were all their lifetime subject to bondage. For verily he took not on him the nature of angels; but he took on him the seed of Abraham. Wherefore in all things it behooved him to be made like unto his brethren; that he might be a merciful and faithful high priest in things pertaining to God to make reconciliation for the sins of the people."

☐ To redeem us from all iniquity and cause us to be a people devoted to doing good works. In Titus 2:13-14 it says, "Looking for that blessed hope and the glorious appearing of the great God and our Saviour Jesus Christ; Who gave himself for us that he might redeem us from all iniquity, and purify unto himself a peculiar people, zealous of good works."

☐ **To demonstrate His righteousness**. In Romans 3:25-26 (AMP) it says, "Whom God displayed publicly [before the eyes of the world] as a [life-giving] sacrifice of atonement and reconciliation (propitiation) by His blood [to be received] through faith. This was to demonstrate His righteousness [which demands punishment for sin] because in His forbearance [His deliberate restraint] He passed over the sins previously committed [before Jesus' crucifixion]. It was to demonstrate His righteousness at the present time, so that He would be just and the One who justifies those who have faith in Jesus [and rely confidently on Him as Savior]."

☐ **<u>To bear witness unto the truth</u>**. In John 18:37 & Romans 15:8-9 it says, "…Thou sayest that I am a king. To this end was I born [*for this purpose*] and for this cause came I into the world, that I should bear witness unto the truth. Every one that is of the truth heareth my voice." "Now I say that Jesus Christ was a minister of the circumcision [Jews] for the truth of God; to confirm the promises made unto the fathers: And that the Gentiles might glorify God for his mercy; as it is written, For this cause I will confess to thee among the Gentiles, and sing unto thy name."

☐ **To fulfill the law and the prophets**. In Matthew 5:17 it says, "Think not that I am come to destroy the law or the prophets; I am not come to destroy, but to fulfil."

☐ **To bring peace and unity**. In Ephesians 2:14-18 (AMP) it says, "For He Himself is our peace and our bond of unity. He who made both groups – [Jews and Gentiles] – into one body and broke down the barrier and the dividing wall [of spiritual antagonism between us] by abolishing in His [own crucified] flesh the hostility caused by the law with its commandments contained in ordinances [which He satisfied]; so that in Himself He might make the two into one new man, thereby establishing peace. And [that He] might reconcile them both [Jew and Gentile, united] in one body to God through the cross, thereby putting to death the hostility. And He came and preached the good news of peace to you [Gentiles] who were far away and peace to those [Jews] who were near. For it is through Him that we both have a [direct] way of approach in one Spirit to the Father."

☐ **To preach the gospel of the kingdom**. In Luke 4:18-19, 42-43 it says, "The Spirit of the Lord is upon me, because he hath anointed me to preach the gospel to the poor; he hath sent me to heal the brokenhearted, to preach deliverance to the captives and recovering of sight to the blind; to set at liberty them that are bruised to preach the acceptable year of the Lord." And when it was day, he departed and went into a desert place: and the people sought him, and came unto him, and stayed him, that he should not depart from them, And he said unto them, I must preach *the kingdom of God* to other cities also: for therefore am I sent."

☐ **To call sinners to repentance**. In Mark 2:17 it says, "When Jesus heard it, he saith unto them, They that are whole have no need of the physician, but they that are sick: I came not to call the righteous, but sinners to repentance."

☐ **To destroy the works of the devil**. In 1 John

3:8 it says, "He that committeth sin is of the devil; for the devil sinneth from the beginning. *For this purpose,* the Son of God was manifested, that he might destroy the works of the devil."

☐ **To serve [minister] and give his life a ransom for many**. In Mark 10:45 it says, "For even the son of man came not to be ministered unto, but to minister and to give his life a ransom for many."

☐ **To die**. In John 12:24-27 it says, "Verily, verily, I say unto you, Except a corn of wheat fall into the ground and die, it abideth alone: but if it dies, it bringeth forth much fruit. He that loveth his life shall lose it; and he that hateth his life in this world shall keep it unto life eternal. If any man serve me, let him follow me and where I am, there shall also my servant be; if any man serve me, him will my Father honour. Now is my soul troubled and what shall I say? Father, save me from this hour: but *for this cause came I* unto this hour."

☐ **To glorify the Father in the earth. In** John 17:4

it says, "I have glorified thee on the earth: I have finished the work, which thou *gavest me to do.*

All of these things were being manifested, as purpose, through Jesus Christ and his ministry. Some of them extend to us in our purpose as the elect in the earth, but we also have specific purposes assigned by the Father as well. It is our responsibility to grow in intimacy with the Father and come to know and aggressively pursue our purpose, making it the drive of our life. Jesus said it this way, "My meat [strength nourishment /sustenance] is to do the will of him that sent me and to finish his work (John 4:34)." His focus was totally devoted to completing what God had assigned him to do and making sure he was always pleased by his actions. Our commitment should be the same, to obey the Father by fulfilling what we were created for.

The Final work...

We now understand fully what Christ was assigned to accomplish in the earth and we can see his commitment and dedication to the Father as an obedient son. All his ministry work culminated to the "grand finale" with Christ dying on the cross, visiting those in the grave with the gospel and taking the keys "authority" from the devil and then "conquering death" and being resurrected after (Matt. 27:32-56; Mark 15:21-37; Luke 23:26-46; John 19:17-30; John 5:28; 1Pet. 4:6; Heb. 2:14-15; Rom. 6:9; 1Cor. 15:26, 54-55).

We see Jesus acknowledging that he had accomplished the prerequisites of the final act in John 19:28-30. It says, "...Jesus *knowing that all things were now accomplished*, that the scripture might be fulfilled, saith I thirst. Now there was set a vessel full of vinegar: and they filled a sponge with vinegar and put it upon hyssop and put it to his mouth. When Jesus therefore had received the vinegar, *he said, It is finished*: and he bowed his head, and gave up the ghost."

Finally, through several scriptures we are made aware of the fullness of Christ's victory and the fullness of His preeminence over all things, including and specifically death. In Colossians 2:18-20 it says, "[he] is the head of the body, the church: who is the beginning, the *firstborn from the dead*; that in all things he might have the preeminence. For it pleased the Father that in him should all fullness dwell; having *made peace through the blood of his cross, by him to reconcile [restore] all things unto himself*; by him, I

say, whether they be things in earth, or things in heaven."
The last enemy to be abolished and put to an end [was]
death, and Christ obtained *"dominion over death"* and the
scripture [is] fulfilled that says, '*death is swallowed up in
victory* [vanquished forever]' (Romans 6:9; 1Cor. 15:26, 54-
55). Hebrews 2:14-15 puts it this way, *"...through death he
might destroy him that had the power of death, that is, the
devil*; and deliver them who through fear of death were all
their lifetime subject to bondage." The Lord has
triumphantly won the victory, reconciled both the kingdom
and those who were enslaved by the original kingdom
seizure (Genesis 3), *defeated the devil and spoiled [all]
principalities and powers, he made a shew of them openly,
triumphing over them in [his victory and defeat of death]*
(Col. 2:14-15). In Revelation 1:18 Christ tells John, "...I
died, but see, *I am alive forevermore, and I have the keys of
[absolute control and victory over] death and of Hades* (the
realm of the dead)." In John 5:27-29 (AMP) Jesus said it this
way, "[the Father] has given Him authority to execute
judgment because He is a Son of Man [sinless humanity,
qualifying Him to sit in judgment over mankind]. Do not be
surprised at this; for a time is coming when *all those who
are in the tombs will hear His voice, and they will come out –*

105

those who did good things [will come out] to a resurrection of [new] life, but those who did evil things [will come out] to a resurrection of judgment [that is, to be sentenced]." Listen when Jesus said "it is finished" he was declaring to us that he had done a complete work, satisfying all that had been taken out of the way and realigning all things with the original will and plan of the Father. What we have received in him is complete [perfectness], and in full alignment with his victory; in that it manifests in our modern day lives the same as it did with those in the early church. As born-again believers we *can* "see [conceptualize and manifest]" the kingdom of God.

Our submission to his kingship legally affords us transmission of rights, privileges, etc. We ARE his church, the ekklesia: the called-out ones, a royal priesthood, a holy nation, those meant to house and display the wonderful deeds and virtues and perfections of Him who afforded us this new state of being (1Peter2:4-5,9; 1Cor. 3:16-17; 6:5-20; 12:27; 2Cor. 6:16-18; Eph. 1:22; 2:19-22; 4:15-16; Gal. 3:26-29). The Lord is waiting for you to show up in power, like Jesus, as a true son/daughter!

PART FOUR:

ADDITIONAL FOUNDATION: BIBLICAL STRUCTURES

CHAPTER 10

WHY 5 GIFTS OF CHRIST

Everything that the Lord does has specific purposes and nothing in His kingdom is left wanting. He has made provisions for us all to be made "whole [unified/oneness/sound]" "perfect [complete/ mature]" fully "grow[n] up into him in all things" (Ephesians 4:13-15). It is to this end that he has "[given] some, apostles; and some prophets; and some, evangelists; and some pastors and teachers (Ephesians 4:11). Five   empowered diverse leadership officials [officers], "gifts," [trainers/ equippers] to be responsible for carrying out this growth process to those "delivered from the power of [the kingdom] of darkness and translated into [His] kingdom (Col. 1:13)." When Jesus Christ walked the earth and accomplished his "ministry [service]" to the disciples he operated demonstratively in all the five offices for their perfecting and as an example.

The modern church belonging to Jesus Christ, our

collective communities, should be like a strong discipleship training institute with branches all over the world and with *all* five of these "gifts" [officers/instructors] each operating in their specifications *alongside one another* without competition as we see in the early church. Having standardization in curriculum; the basics of believership for kingdom living in the earth. All of our military forces initiate a new soldier with basic training and a foundation before ever moving them onto "specialty" or occupational training. A part of that foundation is understanding the hierarchical (leadership) structure of rank and responsibility and gaining an honor for the system.

Our great God has a system, a hierarchical (leadership) structure as well and we see it in the first natural church (the family) and in the spiritual church (the holy nation: ekklesia). Those of us who are yoked to Christ would agree that a healthy "whole" godly household is made up of a **father** and **mother**, at its **foundation** and then **children** with each operating in obedience to the leadership of the **Lord Jesus** and the succession of the leadership structure; all for the glory and pleasure of God. According to 1 Corinthians 11:3, "**Christ** is the head of every **man** and the head of every **woman** is the man, and the head of Christ is **God** (paraphrased)," this example reflects levels or tiers of leadership.

We see this leadership model shown again in Ephesians 2:19-20, "... [in] the household of God; and are built upon the *foundation* of the *apostles* and *prophets*, *Jesus Christ* himself being the chief corner stone; in whom all the building fitly framed together groweth unto a holy temple *in the Lord* [Christ]: In whom ye also are builded together *for* a habitation of *God through the Spirit*." As we see, God never lacks structure, systems of operations, principles, and processes to ensure the highest levels of efficiency. There is always a chief leading first officer under Christ's administration (i.e., husbands and apostles) and then there is a secondary officer (i.e., wives and prophets) supporting the first, with Christ solidifying the "foundation" or platform by which everything must stand upon.

In both structures the first officer gets their orders directly from Christ and mirrors and disseminates that information through the secondary officers, who are highly endowed with skills to convey it both effectively and powerfully to produce outcomes through those set to receive (i.e., children, members in the body, the nation). If we really look at this, we can see where we as a body of Christ have mismanaged our responsibilities, refused and rejected God's divine order and even flat out ignored it. We cannot resent God's leadership structure. Let us look at one more example of this divine order of leadership before we move to unpack the roles of the entire 5 gifts of Christ.

In 1 Corinthians 12:4-6 it says, "Now there are diversities of *gifts*, but the same *Spirit*. And there are differences of *administrations*, but the same *Lord*. And there are diversities of *operations*, but it is the same *God* which worketh all in all." God the Father establishes "operations" and an exertion of power or influence; efficacy, potency, principles, processes, and systems that create the highest levels of efficiency when followed. Our Lord Jesus reigns in "administrations" which is the execution and management of public affairs; a governmental agency or board, along with ensuring the efficient performance of all these departments [five-fold officers] in the organization called the "body of Christ" or "bride of Christ." The Holy Spirit oversees the distribution of "gifts" or notable capacity (endowments: power, quality, or attributes). Operations, administrations, and gifts defined by Merriam-Webster.

"God has placed [ordained] and arranged the parts in the body, each one of them, just as He willed and saw fit [with the best balance of function]" (1Cor. 12:18 AMP). In Numbers 18:6 it says, "... I have taken your brethren, the Levites, from among the children of Israel: to you they are given as *a gift* for the Lord; *to do service* of the tabernacle of the congregation." Christ "only [has done], in giving these five *gifts*, what He has seen his father do" place a structure of leadership *"to do service"* and accomplish His desired outcomes (John 5:19; 8:28; Num. 18:6).

Apostles...

As we saw the first gift given by Christ in Ephesians 4:11 was "some apostles." These front-runners are "fathers at heart," meaning they carry the heart of the father and impart identity as received from Christ and the Father. Apostles are also "order- setters" and "authority and standard bearers;" they have vision [architects] for God's building, the temple [building and people] and how they are to exist based on the heavenly model. Foundation layers (1Cor. 3:10). This nature, in and of itself, can at times seem difficult to deal with, even as naturally, many children often seek out mothers first to potentially evade the waves of authority, structure, order and discipline that succinctly flow from this officer. Without a doubt they are "diplomats" and "ambassadors" of the kingdom of God, righteously conveying and portraying it [the kingdom] to the kings/brethren in the earth (God's holy nation 1Pet. 2:9). Insomuch as they not only establish the kingdom of God in regions, but they train up and establish leaders as well, ensuring all that they have been given to do maintains its integrity by visiting and strengthening houses [communities] and the set [local] leadership as needed (Acts 15:36; 14:21-23; Titus 1:5).

They generally have extensive knowledge bases, are problem-solvers, and are resourceful to those connected to them, which is duly given based on the assignment. The complexity of their nature deems support from the prophets. We see this partnership in Exodus 4:15-16 with Aaron supporting Moses, as well as with Zerubbabel, the son of Shealtiel and Jeshua, son of Jozadak, who were set to rebuild the house of God and the prophets of God were helping them in Ezra 5:2. These are both Old Testament examples of apostolic prophetic teams in function, although not specifically called such verbatim. In the New Testament we see Judas (surnamed Barsabas) and Silas accompanying

Paul and Barnabas in Acts 15:22, 25, 27, 32. As the Lord seeks to prepare His "spotless" bride, apostles are a necessary component in setting things in proper order and alignment just as a father brings those elements to the home.

Prophets...

Prophets, like apostles, are tasked with ensuring "[God's] kingdom comes, [and] will [is] being done, on earth as it is in heaven" (Matt. 6:10). These two are foundational authorities. Remember the apostle's thrust is the kingdom, the throne of God, the authority, and the heavenly [deep mysteries and exceptional wisdom]. Whereas, the prophet's thrust of that mandate is the will of God being done, the practical connection of the heavenly [kingdom] into the earthly [assignment]; the "how to" or "Cliff notes [summaries]" and "parts" verses the entire blueprint (1Cor. 13:9). The enforcer of sorts, like how a mother enforces the will of the father in the home.

Both officers come with a heavy dose of authority and truth (i.e., Father *and* Mother). Although I'm making a correlation with natural parentage as a similitude, the offices are *not* gender specific, more so focusing on the balance of power and authority to be a foundation. Furthermore, prophets are designed as premier orators and carriers [wombs] of God's will. They tend to know what He wants and what He doesn't want. They also function in somewhat of a "quality control" manner, as they did not establish it [the work/community /nation], but they examine, judge, and speak to the state of it based solely on the express word and will of God to maintain its designated integrity. At the core, they work to reveal [unveil], determine [assess/quantify] and aid [contribute] in the overall knowledge base of the born-again believer, while admonishing them in submission, obedience *to* and enforcement of God's desired will for the kingdom and their individual life. The whole goal being explicit competency in kingdom capabilities to be within and among the people of God. Like apostles, prophets can be complex and often misunderstood individuals. Nonetheless, these two officers are expressly built by God for the calling through much trial and hardship, ensuring both their fortitude and allegiance.

I want to point out just a few more characteristics of these foundational officers so that you may know what to expect from them, especially since many people are only now becoming familiar with these officers with their resurgence. Apostles are seen throughout scriptures carrying out an "overseeing" type of responsibility, just as a natural father has this responsibility for his family. Apostles provide vision and structure, wisdom, spiritual strength, counsel, rebuke and correction and delegations of authority. They most often carry out the basis of these responsibilities in multiple places, as it is an ambassadorial role in the kingdom. They dispense this blueprint to the regions they have been assigned to by God. They do *not* have to be "invited" because they are delegates of Christ's kingdom *sent* by Him. We often fail to comprehend this dynamic since in our Western culture we have lacked kingdom understanding and have been diverted from these biblical standards of operation. The apostolic prophet (i.e., Judas/Silas) can also go from place to place, as they often accompany apostles (Acts 11:27; 15:32; 18:5). However, we also see in scripture that God always has "house" prophets who are specifically assigned to a community; as seen with many of the Old Testament prophets. In the New Testament as seen in Luke 2:36-38, Anna "did not depart from the temple" and we also see in Acts 13:1 "there were prophets in the church." Keep in mind prophets are similar in role as wives, by which they remain enforcers of their overseers wishes even in their absence.

117

Evangelists…

Evangelists aren't seen as prominently in scripture by title, as the literal word is only listed three times (Acts 21:8; 2Tim. 4:5; & Eph. 4:11). However, they are not less present or less valuable. We need evangelists. They are zealous to spread [herald] the gospel of salvation through Jesus Christ and are those that we see "snatching some from the fire" (Jude 23); meaning their hearts burn in this regard that they aggressively pursue this specific purpose and flow from this grace. They are often the bridge for people to transfer from death to life; avid soul winners. The fact that they are "go-tellers" verses "go-teachers" they are known to keep it moving; ensuring the gospel of Jesus Christ and salvation are ever being told. We know Philip was an evangelist (Acts 21:8) and one of the seven who were chosen as deacons (Acts 21:8 & Acts 6). These deacons were "full of faith, the Holy Ghost, and wisdom" and were known to be working miracles and wonders among the people as a "precursor" to the actual salvation of many. Wisdom, signs, and wonders were most often used for those who did not believe in order to convince them of the greatness of our God (John 4:48; Matt. 12:38-39; Luke 11:29-30; Luke 23:8; John 2:18, 6:30; 1Cor. 1:22-24). True evangelists typically have these as strong earmarks in their ministry, even though all 5 gifts/officers can also manifest them. In fact, we all are encouraged to do this from our "measure of [evangelistic] grace" and Paul encourages Timothy and us to do it in 2Tim. 4:5.

Keep in mind Jesus says, "a disciple (which we all are to be) is not above his master [teacher], but everyone that is perfected (when he is fully trained) shall be *as* his master (like his teacher) (Luke 6:40)." The purpose of all of these "gifts of Christ [teachers/ instructors]" is to perfect (mature) each of us that we may *all* do "the work of the ministry" at our designated grace measure (Eph. 4:12)."

Pastors...

This is the most familiar officer and an awesome one for sure, yet clarification must be given on their role. There has been a "paradigm of the pastor" as the chief leading officer of the church for as long as I can remember, even though the Lord has always had remnants of his church working in right order. Surprising to some, pastors are *NOT* the leading officers of Christ's administration. I know this is a shock to many because it is what has most often been personified. Remember, the church is "built upon the foundation of the apostles and prophets, not upon the pastors (Eph. 2:20-22; 3:5). Pastors, in fact, are similar to elders in that they *are mainstays* (Acts 14:23). They are to be mature and seasoned in the word of truth and able to rehearse those truths with those within the church, the body of Christ. Yet I must reiterate, as I know this falsity runs deep; they are *NOT* the standard bearers or chief authority as many had perceived. It is just not scriptural as we saw that it's the apostle and prophet that hold these specific "foundational" and "front-runner" functions for Christ's administrative team. However, we do see them working *with* apostles throughout the New Testament (Acts 15:2, 4, 6, 22-23; 16:4).

Jeremiah, the prophet, speaks extensively on the pastor, but notice it is from a position of authority (a prophet relaying God's mind) and much of it is in rebuke to their misuse of the office. In Jeremiah 10:21 he says, "[they] are become brutish (stupid/irrational /unreceptive/ grossly sensual) and have not sought the Lord." In Jeremiah 12:10 he says, "many pastors have destroyed [his] vineyard, they have trodden my portion underfoot, they have made [his] pleasant portion a desolate wilderness." Then in Jeremiah 23:1-2 he says, "woe be unto the pastors that destroy and scatter the sheep of my pasture...ye have scattered my flock, and driven them away, and have not visited them: behold I will visit upon you the evil of your doings." In all these places we see where the pastors were "out of order" and we see this today where many have deviated from God's original plan and purpose for their office. The greatest responsibility of the pastor is to "lead [be an example to]" the sheep, but what should be understood is that it's not on a new path or in new doctrine, but the one that has been laid by the apostles (Acts 2:41-42). A sound example of this working is in Exodus 18:17-26 where we see Moses, who is an Old Testament apostle type, needing to delegate authority to able men, such as fear God, men of truth, and [that] hate covetousness.

Essentially, this is the setting of "elders/pastors" to shepherd or pastor the church (people) (1Peter 5:1- 3; Acts 20:17, 28). It is truly clear both in the Old & New Testaments that pastors are to be working *with* and *under* the leadership [oversight] of apostles.

Remember, these are Christ's administrative officers with similar relation as in the secular arena to the relationship and roles of store manager [pastor] verses a regional or general manager [apostle].

Hence, the issues we see Jeremiah rebuking were due to a lack of oversight from an apostolic voice. In the New Testament, we consistently see Peter and Paul giving counsel and wisdom to the pastors (elders) who were left to shepherd (lead) the churches in their absence, as they continued to travel and establish and confirm the many gatherings of disciples in various regions. In the past, I have also used the analogy of pastors being liken unto nurses in the maternity ward of a hospital. They do not "birth" the babies per se, but they are the essential caregivers who tend to them while the mother is recovering and until they are able to advance to home life. They could also be related to as similar to primary teachers, who constantly rehearse the fundamentals with the student until they move on to high school where they are expected to have learned in a way that now enables a more independent work model. They *are* vital in watching over and teaching the fundamentals of the new birth and tenets thereof.

The truth is that many pastors, like single mothers, have merely done the best that they could with the knowledge and understanding that they had, but without the presence of fathers (apostles) there's surely imbalance, lack of discipline and identity crisis within the house, among the children of God. The same as we see it manifest in natural fatherless homes; first that which is natural then that which is spiritual (1Cor. 15:46). Lastly, in this office, I want to reiterate that they are vitally important and valuable and the only reason I am needing to share correction is because they have been the most out of order and in the greatest rejection of God's apostles as the leading officer, yet they have read all these truths in their own bibles. Nevertheless, "the Lord disciplines and corrects those whom he loves (Heb. 12:6 AMP)." He loves the pastors and so do we.

Teachers...

Teachers are just that, instructors, which have very diligently studied and can rightly divide the word of truth, including the historical context. They have a special grace measure to do so. They are great expounders of the word of truth. They are mentioned thirdly in 1 Cor. 12:28 and we do see this role specifically attached to both apostles and prophets in other scriptures. Understandably, as you cannot very well be one to bring foundation and not be able to teach that which you are carrying: the kingdom and the will ofGod.

Paul calls himself a teacher in 1 Tim. 2:7 & 2 Tim. 1:11, and in Acts 13:1 they are connected to the prophets. They are listed last in the five officers captured in the Ephesians 4:11 text, but that is not a diminishment of their role. This role in the five-fold has a special designation of authority as with the other four offices, "gifts" of Christ. As we know, universally people can be teachers of many things and we all "should be teachers" based on Hebrews 5:12. However, this teacher of Christ has a capability of exception in teaching on His word, will and purposes for mankind in the earth and in context of the Holy Scriptures. Most often, teachers are well versed on the historical timelines, settings, and cultural climate of the accounts in scripture.

Based on 2 Tim.2:15, we should all "study to show ourselves approved, able to rightly divide the word of truth (paraphrased) and according to Ephesians 4:7, "every one of us is given grace according to the measure of the gift of Christ." If we relate it back to the military example, we are all on *a* level (operating in *a* grace) and just not all in the same station/ ranking of service. A key element I want to emphasize, even in using the military example, is that the varying degree/grace has everything to with authority/rank, but we should *all* be operating from our kingdom/royal position and ministering: proclaiming and promoting the kingdom by dismantling the king of darkness off people's lives, setting at liberty those who are captive.

Keep in focus that all the Ephesians 4:11 officers, "the apostles, prophets, evangelists, pastors, and teachers are for the perfecting of the saints [so] they [the saints] can [do] the work of the ministry for the edifying [building/instruction] of the body of Christ" "that we be no more children [unskilled and immature] tossed to and fro, and carried about with every wind of doctrine (Eph. 4:11, 14)." These are all teachers, they are not to be idolized or worshipped, and they are not even good at their jobs if the saints are *not* becoming skillful and matured. As a whole, we are slacking and can in no way brag because the current state of the church is embarrassing. Overall, it operates impotent, weak, and ineffectively. We must get back on track doctrinally and operate within the order/ structure and systems the Lord had originally set in order to become what he originally intended: kings and priest after the order of Christ (Rev. 1:6).

In closing, I want us to remember that all these officers are "brethren" whom have just been given responsibilities in the body "to serve [work]" for the Lord, and Christ is our only master (Matt. 23:8). The body of Christ must move from idolizing and coveting these functions. We cannot all be the eye, we cannot all be the ear or the hand, but we must all humbly carry out *whatever* responsibilities Christ has assigned us to. Christ is Lord of all, and we are *many brethren* (Acts 10:36, 2:36; Phil. 2:9-11; Rom. 14:9, 8:29).

CHAPTER 11

IS CHURCH ESSENTIAL OR NOT?

ccording to an article by Jeffrey Jones posted in the politics section of Gallup, a global analytic firm, U.S. church membership has been sharply declining over the past two decades. There was only half of the American population that were church members as of 2019, which is down from it previously being at a 70% rate. It further states that the decline is mostly attributed to an increase of the percentage of people who are claiming *no religious affiliation*. Jones says, "Given that church membership and religiosity in general is greater among older adults, the emergence of an increasingly secular generation to replace far more religious older generations suggests the decline in the U.S. church membership overall *will continue*."

I want to begin by first establishing that so many truths of the bible have been erroneously taught and have been used to manipulate the people of God. In the case of church membership, we have handled it wrong, and most leaders have not righteously and with great diligence sought to work as one body.

Although we may be in various regions, we haven't put enough emphasis on us being "one body" so therefore we just don't intentionally work to this end. According to Romans 12:5, *"we, [though] being many, are one body in Christ and everyone members one of another."* In 1 Cor. 12:27, it says, *"now we are the body of Christ and members in particular."* Why then do we have so many leaders who condemn and oppress born-again believers, who remain in the body, but fellowship with many churches? We have antagonized and condemned the saints unnecessarily. Does one not have the right to associate with their "family" in other gatherings?

Why do we have leaders in the body who resist working with other leaders in the body? Is it rooted in fear? Is it being respecters of persons [showing favoritism]? Surely, we all know that there are false prophets and other leaders but are we who are true *not* discerning? We do not seem to know how to "bear one another" as we are instructed in scripture (Eph. 4:2-6; Col. 3:12-15). It seems we forget that simply we are better and stronger *together*. Strong communities are the bedrock for a stronger people. The erosion of biblical standards in our country and throughout society have directly affected people and have falsely liberated them to believe anything goes. The breakdown in turn affects the church and unfortunately its current leadership regimes. We saw that the five gifts [officers] of Christ are supposed to be working together in this great venture of building a strong nation of people for God according to scripture (Eph. 4:11-16). So, why are the functions and manifestations of the Holy Spirit of the early churches not in operation in our modern-day churches? Has God changed? Or have we changed? Considering these things, I think that most spiritual leaders today would attest to these statistics we read to be true. Church membership is declining, and people are embracing secularism by the groves. Things have changed. Many people who are still "with God" have grown frustrated with the corrupted leadership and systems by which we operate "church" in this day and time; they have also opted out of it. I believe that some of them have done so at God's instruction to back away rather than to becomebitter.

Divisions, unbiblical practices, cliques, worldliness, unhealed leaders, unhealed laity, and lots of traditions of men have not drawn us closer to God and have not produced the "revival" or "move of God" that we attest to desire. Yet, I am optimistic. My optimism isn't hinged on worldly assessments, but on the nature and historic patterns of God. I know God and I know that when there are issues, He has always got the answers. Now that we've had to deal with some of our "dirty laundry," let us dive in to answer the million-dollar question. "Is church essential or not?"

In the history of the bible, we do not see church as quite the same institution as we see today. First, the word *'church'* does not even appear in the Old Testament. Now, I hear some of you immediately saying, "but they had the temple." I want to let you know that was David's idea, not God's idea (2Sam. 7:1-2). With Adam and Eve, God met with them in the cool of the day (Gen. 3:8).

With Noah, Abraham, and Moses we see God also just presenting himself directly to them and speaking to them openly. He even tells David that he has never done the temple thing (2Sam7:6). In all those conversations the focus was a "nation of people" and a "people for Himself;" "a family" and "community" of holy kingdom-focused [peculiar] people *NOT* a building. From the beginning until now, God's highest interest is and has always been relationship. Relationship was and still is HIS focus. Now, we must understand that the context of relationships affords those we love privilege. God isn't different. God never asked for a church/temple, but it was David's idea, rooted in guilt, that he himself had a "house" and the ark was housed in a tent (2Sam. 7:1-2). David wanted to honor God for His goodness and faithfulness and *desired* to build God a temple. God, in love and kindness, honored David's desire. He just said that David could not do it himself, but that his seed could after he dies (2Sam. 7:12-13). Even in this situation if you study it, God did a greater thing in not just allowing David his request, but immediately begins to talk to him about covenant of an eternal future with his lineage. Our God is a God of relationship, which is not one-sided, but hinged on divine exchange; pleasing one another and covenants [agreements with promises and benefits attached].

Fast forward to our modern times, we can see that we have spent tremendous efforts "majoring in the minors and minoring in the majors" so to speak. What I mean is that much of the efforts of the current leadership regime has not been hinged on the heart of God, on relationship, or on establishing God's reign [domination] in every sphere of the earth by His kings [us/the redeemed]. It has been on self-serving acts and on the accolades and approval of men. We see all the props though, the externals, the lights, the cameras and all the branding and visual appearances. In and of themselves, they are not bad, but when we can't even detect God's will, God's presence, or God's approval upon most of it, then it's off. We do not see the power of God manifested as in times of old, nor do we see doctrinal soundness, and no emphasis is placed on kingdom affiliation. Instead, the focus of many leaders is on *their* church or *their* denomination affiliation, and not the church of Jesus Christ. Please understand I am not saying every leader, or every church is corrupted, or that it's wrong to identify what community or clan we are a part of. However, way too many have veered off course, and since we are *"one body"* if one is affected, we all are affected.

As we study the scriptures, we know that God *always* gets what He wants. Anytime people were inhibitors to the nation [people] of God living, loving, and serving Him in righteousness, He would move to deal harshly with them, even if it were the very people themselves: exiled. Adam and

Eve were put out of the garden (Genesis 3:23-24). Noah and his 7 family members were all that survived the wickedness of his time as God flooded the earth (Genesis 6-10). Abraham and his family were preserved upon Sodom and Gomorrah's destruction by brimstone and fire (Genesis 19:24-25). Moses watched Pharaoh and his Egyptian army destroyed by the Red sea (Exodus 14). In Exodus 19:6, we see God reiterating *His desire* saying, "and ye shall be unto me *a kingdom of priests and a holy nation.*"

You must recall all that has been written in the previous chapters concerning the kingdom of God and the purposes of Christ, and *that* being God's will. God is consistent, He has not changed His mind or desire to this day. Christ came, took on flesh, overcame sin death and the grave, accomplishing the great plan for the redemption and restoration of the kingdom and all the kingdom constituents [us]. Dare we ignore our new life, all its endowments and our role in God's big picture?

Should we just keep "doing church" as usual and think we will not kindle God's anger? I pray not. What I want you to do now is pause and consider the present times. As I write this book, the entire world has been put on a "time out" and instructed to "shelter in place [at home]" during this COVID-19 Pandemic of 2020. Churches across the globe have been closed *along* with businesses. Is God moving to have His way once more? Everything about this says, "Yes!" There *must* be a restructuring of how we live, love on, and worship our God going forward.

During Jesus' ministry and the early church, they gathered "in the temple *and* from house to house" "not forsaking the assembling of [themselves] together and living lives *immersed* in spreading the gospel and honoring God's will (Acts 5:42; Heb. 10:25)." Becoming communities of those committed to His righteous will being done in the earth is our priority. So, the answer is "church" the ekklesia (the called-out ones) are most certainly *essential*; now more than ever. It is us, the kings and priest of Christ's lineage that are essential and it's vitally important that we operate in unity and stand in the fullness of our dominion that we have been given by Christ in his finished work to reign on the earth like never before (Rev. 5:10, 1:6; 1Pet. 2:9). It is not time to shrink back but to rise up and reign. We cannot return to gathering in the ways of the past, in futility. Church cannot just be another entertainment venue, operating like social clubs, and spiritual brothels where people pay to get their weekly "fix," or even modern day "dens of thieves" where there's just buying, selling, and handling of all the "business of the church." This is not acceptable to God and will not be tolerated in this "reset." Woe unto those who attempt to maintain this hypocrisy (John 2:13-16; Matt. 23).

According to 1 John 2:15, "[we must] love *not* the world, neither the things that are in the world... for all that is in the world, the lust of the flesh and the lust of the eyes and the pride of life, is not of the Father, but is of the world." It is high time that we "bring forth fruits meet for repentance" (Matt. 3:8). We must resume gathering with renewed purpose and as Dr. Paula Price says, "[be] scripturally organic and culturally unmodified" exhorting one another in this hour more than ever as the day approaches (qtd. Price) (Heb. 10:25). May the brethren, the heirs, the true church of Jesus Christ rise!

CHAPTER 12

SPIRITUAL FATHERS VS. TEACHERS

"I write not these things to shame you, but as my beloved **sons** I warn you. For though ye have ten thousand **instructors** in Christ, yet have ye not many **fathers**: for in Christ Jesus, I have **begotten** you through the gospel (1Cor. 4:14-15)." It is expanded in the Message Bible to say, "There are a lot of people around who can't wait to tell you what you've done wrong, but there aren't many fathers willing to take the time and effort to help you grow up. It was as Jesus helped me proclaim God's Message to you that I became your father (1Cor.4:15 MSG)."

I want to begin by first outlining the definitions of some of these key words seen in the scripture above, as it will bring greater understanding in the text ahead. These words are those that I've highlighted and emphasized in the text above.

☐ **Sons**: offspring, children as produced; the name transferred to that intimate and reciprocal relationship formed between men (persons) by the bonds of love and trust as between parents and children

☐ **Instructors**: a tutor, instructor, schoolmaster; one who teaches something (i.e., teacher, professor, rabbi, etc.)

☐ **Fathers**: a male parent, ancestor, especially the founder of a family or line; progenitor; to *beget,* to be the creator, founder or author of; originate

☐ **Begotten**: of men who fathered children; to engender, cause to arise, excite; to convert someone; procreate; regenerate (regrow; replace loss or injury of); bring forth

☐ **Mentor (not listed but I thought important to identify the difference from instructor/teacher)**: an experienced and trusted counselor/adviser or teacher; advise or train (especially a younger colleague; typically, in a specific area of expertise)

Paul makes it very clear to us, from a stance of warning, that this is definitely something that would be problematic; that throughout the journey of a life with Jesus many will come, instruct and mentor, but they will not by reason of this dilemma assume the position of being your father, your "birther" nor have the credibility and authority by which you are to use as the "standard" for any major adjustments in your walk; so as not to be "tossed to and fro" and deceived (Eph. 4:14). Reflecting on Chapter 9, we understand that apostles are "fathers at heart" and in their spiritual operation they carry the heart of the father and impart identity as received from Christ and the Father. No one else can actually give you your identity other than your father, the one who carried you as a seed in their loins (either naturally or spiritually). I want to insert that I'm not saying only apostles can father, as the apostolic *grace* [not office] is upon all who father/birth. Paul does make it very clear though that we may have as many as "ten thousand" instructors. In essence, our learning is not hinged upon one person. Throughout life in general and as it relates to spiritual matters, we will learn and glean from many who are more advanced in whatever area of study, but they'll never have the authority to "rewrite" our lineage.

Here are some clear distinctions:

☐ **Teachers** spend time in study and then merely disseminate that information; **Fathers** pour out their lives expending everything (money, time, and energy), and their primary method of teaching is through modeling excellence and imparting wisdom for their children, both natural and spiritual (2Cor. 12:15).

☐ **Teachers** are more motivated by illumination (mere enlightenment); **Fathers** are motivated by personal transformation; they want to see it manifested: fruit.

Therefore, they will walk with you, correct you, encourage you and aid you in your life's journey in order to maximize your full potential. **Fathers** become both one's greatest advocate *and* coach.

☐ **Teachers** are in search for students to give them temporary satisfaction of releasing their prized *knowledge, information, and insights* to;

Fathers are in search for lifetime connection, sons and daughters, to groom and build leadership within, whom they can pour *themselves* into for duplication and legacy

☐ **Teachers** are innumerable in one's life as you have family members (grandparents, aunts, uncles, siblings, etc.), then you have all your school teachers (primary, secondary, and higher education) counselors and administrators who will all emphatically impart and affect your life at some measure; **Fathers** are different in that there's usually only a few who stand out significantly that took exceptional time out and didn't just deposit something, but worked with you nurturing it until it grew into maturity and was producing "fruit" in your life

☐ **Teachers** have joy and satisfaction if you capture and learn the specific area of study that they have worked with you on; **Fathers** have joy and satisfaction in your life's success as they understand knowledge alone doesn't make one successful, but it must be coupled with wisdom and enactments that produce victories to ensure the accomplishment of destiny. It also becomes a part of their legacy.

☐ **Teachers** are excited when they have deep intellectual connection with their students. Oftentimes, the satisfaction is connected to their disseminated knowledge being the prized component not the student; **Fathers** have a heart connection with their children and the "prized component" is you. You are their pride and joy, seeing you come into a place of maturity and purpose brings deep satisfaction to the father.

☐ **Teachers** desire opportunity to teach so much so that most love it in a way that they'd do it for free. They love their platform and their pride is in their knowledge and ability to disseminate it;

Fathers seek opportunity for their sons and daughters to minister (conduct business/attend to assignments), to represent them and show forth their learning and their maturity. Fathers are builders, legacy creators; they think and operate in the sense of long-term outcomes. They want to see the returns on their investment lived out by you the son or daughter. (Mattera, 2018, blog)

The cost of fathering is so high and truly does require the outpouring of the life of the father that many not only don't do it they won't; they refuse to even attempt at it, which leads me to this point; the excessive declaration of all these spiritual fathers and mothers in today's churches is bogus. It's a hoax by "wolves in sheep's clothing" who are exploiting the insecurities of a fatherless and motherless generation (Matt. 7:15). As the inordinate desires for "a following," money, fame and prestige plague our houses of worship, leaders have gone to great lengths to build "kingdoms" (their own, not God's) at the expense of innocent people who are genuinely seeking God, spiritual guidance and familial connection/ relationships.

God very often gives you fathers on two or three different levels. First, in your personal life, natural biological parentage, and if they are absent, he may use others to fulfill this role. Then He gives one who builds your spiritual foundation. This second father may launch you into your destiny if pride and/or fear and insecurity are not present. Otherwise, there's a third who fashions you and launches you into your destiny/ purpose / ministry work (Taylor 45). Nevertheless, we should be grateful for all the teachers and mentors and should consider ourselves extremely blessed if we get two to three faithful fathers in our lifetime. Surely, we pray that the voices of the prophets will be instrumental in "turn[ing] the heart of the fathers [back] to the children and the heart of the children [back] to their fathers" (Malachi 4:5-6).

CHAPTER 13

TO GIVE OR NOT TO GIVE: MONEY MATTERS

I n this chapter, we are going to talk biblical giving. In the world they say, "money is a mood changer." Unfortunately, we see this statement to be true also in the church. Often, the way we view money, is directly related to our upbringing. What relationship do you have with money? How do you view money? The answer to these questions will determine how you handle it when it comes to God's business.

In Matthew 25:14-30, the "parable of the talents" gives us a good starting point on the expectation that the Lord has on us as it relates to money. It reads:

"For the kingdom of heaven is as a man travelling into a far country, who called his own servants, and delivered unto them his goods. And unto one he gave five talents, to another two, and to another one; to every man according to his several ability; and straightway took his journey. Then he that had received the five talents went and traded with the same and made them other five talents. And likewise, he that had received two, he also gained other two. But he that had received one went and digged in the earth and hid his lord's money. After a long time, the lord of those servants cometh and reckoneth with them. And so, he that had received five talents came and brought other five talents, saying, Lord, thou deliveredst unto me five talents: behold, I have gained beside them five talents more. His Lord said unto him, Well done, thou *good and faithful* servant: thou hast been faithful over a few things, I will make thee ruler over many things; enter thou into the joy of thy lord. He also that had received two talents came and said, Lord, thou deliveredst unto to me two talents: behold, I have gained two other talents beside them.

His lord said unto him, Well done, *good and faithful* servant; thou hast been faithful over a few things, I will make thee ruler over many things: enter thou into the joy of thy lord. Then he which had received the one talent came and said, Lord, I knew thee that thou art a hard man, reaping where thou hast not sown, and gathering where thou hast not strawed: And I was afraid, and went and hid thy talent in the earth: lo, there thou hast that is thine. His lord answered and said unto him, Thou **wicked and slothful** servant; thou knewest that I reap where I sowed not and gather where I have not strawed:

Thou oughtest therefore to have put my money to the exchangers and then at my coming, I should have received mine own with usury [interest/increase]. Take therefore the talent from him, and give it unto him which hath ten talents. For unto everyone that hath shall be given, and he shall have abundance: but from him that hath not shall be taken away even that which he hath. And cast ye the **unprofitable servant** into outer darkness: there shall be weeping and gnashing of teeth.

Here we see a few key points. First, we understand that the expectation is for good stewardship which means both maintenance *and* growth. No one expects to "sow/invest" and not to "reap/harvest" additionally from their investment. Second, I want you to notice in verse 26, the lord calls the person who does not produce anything "wicked and slothful" and rebukes him and then strips him of what he has. Yet, both of the other servants received the same blessing and acknowledgment of being "good and faithful" even though they operated at different measures. Lastly, I want you to notice that the unharvested talent was not given to the one with the least, but to the one with the most.

The principles that we see in this parable reflect the nature of God. When we have a "poverty mindset" our belief system is full of scarcity and "wicked" or low thinking rather than abundance. That mindset thinks that things are hard to get and that money is hard to earn and that there isn't enough out there. T his thinking can come from not having enough as a child or as an adult, but ultimately it comes from the devil. In Luke 19:11-27, this similar parable to the first demands that we are responsible, having good stewardship and multiplying (increasing) what we have been left to steward over. The statement "occupy until I come" literally means to carry on business, the business of a banker or a trader (Luke 19:13). We are to be productive and thriving in all industries. From the beginning when Adam and Eve fell, Satan imputed within mankind sin, sickness, spiritual death and *poverty* (thinking and experientially); these are all the opposites of an eternal abundant life in God as a royal.

In Matthew 21:18-22, we see the instance of Jesus cursing the fig tree for not producing. God's nature is multiplicative, and he made man to "be fruitful and multiply" with every seed producing after its own kind (Gen 1:28; 1:11-12, 21-25; 9:7). Remember, many things are "seeds" and "as long as the earth remains, there will be seed [sowing] time and harvest [reaping] (Gen. 8:22). Therefore, only something or someone in rebellion and opposition to the Lord will not do so (reproduce). Therefore, we see the unproductive servant being called "wicked" in the parable of the talents and that's why we see the fig tree being cursed in the last text we looked at. Now that we understand this principle that we are to be producers and to be "life-bearing" even as our Father in heaven, we can look at giving with a clearer and renewed mind. God's purpose in giving is that there is perpetual provision for *all*. Every time you give, you can and should expect a return because God has instituted this law that governs the earth.

Throughout scripture, we see several types of giving: tithes, first fruits, seeds or offerings, and alms. God has a purpose for everything; he created perfect systems, that if followed, would eradicate all the problems we see in the world today. Sin has done such massive damage in humanity and all the systems surrounding them. If we understand his purposes, we can be more equipped to pursue and perform them. Now let's define these types of giving and learn God's intended purpose for them.

- ☐ **Tithe**: a tenth part; the tenth part of agricultural produce or personal income set apart as an offering to God or for works of mercy or the same amount regarded as an obligation or tax for the support of the church, priesthood, or the like

- ☐ **First Fruit**: first, beginning, best, chief; principal thing; a beginning of sacrifice; to commence; the earliest gathered fruits offered to the Deity in acknowledgment of the gift of fruitfulness

- ☐ **Offering (seed)**: contribution, offering; a present especially in sacrifice or as tribute; gift; something offered, especially a sacrifice ceremonially offered as a part of worship; a contributionto the support of a church

- ☐ **Alms**: mercy, pity; the benefaction itself, a donation to the poor; mercy: kindness or good will towards the miserable and the afflicted, joined with a desire to help them; something such as money or food given freely to relieve the poor; charity

Again, all of these are different types of giving to serve different purposes.

The tithe is considered "holy unto the Lord" and it is given in honor and recognition that He is your provider and that you may remain in reverential fear [awe-inspiring reverence and submission] of the Lord always, but it is established *for* the Levite as compensation for their service, as priests on behalf of the people of God and as a support for the orphans, widows, and strangers [those not a part of the community/ nation] who are among you (Deut. 14:23, 29; Lev. 27:30; Gen. 14:20; Gen 28:20-22; Num. 18:21, 26). Levites were required to tithe also. Tithes were also used for celebrations/feasts.

The first fruit is as simple as it states, it's giving that honors the start or commencement of tithing. You can't tithe unless you are receiving harvests/gain; so, you give the whole first harvest (first fruit) to the Lord in thanksgiving for creating a stream or blessing that you didn't previously have, recognizing that you'll get to keep 90% of each perpetual harvest thereafter where you previously had zero (Deut. 26:1-10; Lev. 23: 9-14; Ex. 23:16, 19; Rom. 11:16). So, if you get a new job, start a new business, etc., a first fruit is warranted as it is a new "land" a new stream of income [harvesting place] that God has brought you into (Prov. 3:9-10).

Offerings, unlike tithes and first fruits, have no specific amount or portion that you must give; it's totally voluntary (2 Cor. 9:7). It is a gift of thanksgiving of gratefulness, a "free-will" offering or a "seed" simply set to create more crops to harvest (1Chron. 29:9; Deut. 16:17; Luke 6:38; Prov. 11:24).

Keep in mind that giving is a form of worship and the more blessed one is, the more value one places on the source [God] of the blessings (Ps. 96:8-9). So, we put a great value on offering as it declares to Him his "worthship (worthiness)" to us.

That last category of alms, also called charity or benevolence, is a form of giving that symbolizes kindness (an attribute of God) as well as the responsibility of being blessed and is very pleasing to the Lord (Heb. 13:16; Prov. 19:17;

28:27; 31:20; Luke 12:33; 10:30-37; 14:12-14. Throughout scripture, God instructs those who are His to take responsibility for those less fortunate among them, both the native and the foreigner (stranger) (Lev. 25:35; Deut. 15:7; Is. 58:7, 10; Matt. 5:42; 25:35-40; Luke 10:35; Eph. 4:28; 1Tim. 6:18; 1John 3:17). Alms are to be done "in secret" to protect the dignity of those experiencing difficulty (Matt. 6:1-4).

It is very clear that God not only is concerned about every person's provision, but that He has instituted systems to enable that provision. For the record, Jesus never "abolished" tithes or any offerings; we only see him rebuking the Pharisees for disproportionate *pride* in their "keeping of this tenet" and not giving enough attention to other "weightier matters" (Matt. 23:23). The tithe remained intact.

In the early church, we do see a bit of a different response to giving, in fact, by the power of the Holy Spirit they upped the ante. In Acts 4:31-37, we see these zealous born-again believers bringing community living to a whole new level, economic empowerment at its finest. It was rooted in "oneness" of heart and soul and invoked through prayer and by the Holy Spirit. While we are here, let's destroy the diabolical practice that has emerged in many modern-day churches. Laying money at the feet of the apostles (or other leadership) is *NOT* a righteous response to "applaud" them; it's rooted in idol worship. The biblical instance of laying money down at the apostles' feet was for *distribution* within their community economy (Acts 4:35). Keep in mind the apostles represented the father, and the kingdom, so laying it at their feet symbolized refusal for God's kingdom, to be in waste (lack). We appreciate when men and women of God bring the word of truth and offerings for their service is acceptable, but let's not give the enemy any place for pride (in them) and idol worship (from us). All of us must be sure to keep our motives pure (Phil. 4:17; Prov. 11:24).

Lastly, I want to deal with honorariums more specifically (a payment rendered for service where custom or propriety *forbids a price to be set*), gifts/ offerings designated for a man or woman of God who is preaching the gospel. It is totally acceptable and scriptural for them (five-fold leaders) to receive monies to enable their service (present and future travels/works) and to have their meals and accommodations paid for (1Cor. 9:11- 14; Gal. 6:6;

1Tim. 5:17-18; Matt. 10:41-42). Christ's servicemen should be able to give themselves fully to prayer and to the ministry of the word" (Acts 6:4). However, it is not acceptable when these exorbitant amounts are charged by some leaders (1Pet. 5:2). It tends to the demonic, in that it fuels greed (love of money which is evil) and it mirrors the exploitation done by the entertainment industry (gauging prices to feed men's lusts) (Matt. 6:24).

Paul, unlike the other apostles, was an *exception* in that he'd often forgo receiving so that it didn't take anything away from the power of his testimony (1Cor. 9:14-18). However, he still affirms that he has a right and that it is acceptable, but his personal choice *not* to receive (1Cor. 9:11-15). In conclusion of this matter, it is both acceptable for leaders *to* receive sustenance from preaching and it's acceptable for them *not to* (which is a choice), but God's system has made provision for them.

"The abundance that this system [God's giving system] was to create, not only kept them "blessed" but was a sign of God being with them and would provoke other nations to envy (Bradley)." In all these things we know, "it is more blessed to give than to receive" and that if we truly "seek first the kingdom of God and his righteousness, [that] all these things [blessings] will be added to [us] (Acts 20:25; Matt. 6:33)."

CONCLUSION

CONCLUSION

I BELIEVE THEREFORE I DO

I n the history of my travels ministering the word of God, both nationally and abroad, I have looked into the faces of people who genuinely want to know God. I really do believe most people want to know God and have an intimate relationship with Him; He made us to long for it. Some are strong believers, some are great in faith, while others can pray impressively. There are also those who reflect the essence of worship precisely, then there's the prudent bible scholars. Some work with the Holy Spirit with such ease and His gifts flow through them flawlessly. We have others who know the kingdom and stand fast in it, some identify with and constantly share Jesus' journey accurately, five-fold gifts have emerged throughout the world at Christ's hand and faithful fathers are rising boldly in righteousness. Kingdom givers, financiers of the gospel, are manifesting from behind the scenes; all are doing these works at the leadership of the Holy Spirit. He leads us, He teaches us, and He convicts and purges us that we bare more fruit (John 16:8, 13; 15:2). The Lord's will and my prayer was not to condemn any, but to lay out clearly the building blocks needed for strength (foundation) in your journey with Jesus Christ and in kingdom living (Eph. 2:20). To pull together the parts that you may have never been discipled and made strong in, that you may have all of what you need (fully equipped). In my introduction I made a lot of strong assertions and I have diligently worked with the Lord's help to clarify each with supporting scriptures and both biblical and modern-day examples of those concepts. The purposes were to spur you on to this point. I challenge you now to *'believe'* and to *'do'* what you have seen and read both here in this book and in the bible verses covered. Rehearse these truths. My prayer is that you use this book as a reference tool to help you fine tune areas where you are strong and to strengthen the areas that you are weak in. Also, use this book to counsel and direct others in that same manner.

We *can be* perfect (strong and mature) and work the ministry (do works/services) to edify (instruct/ improve) the body of Christ until all of us get it and are unified (one/singular) in faith (belief/ conviction) and the knowledge of the Son of God (his life and purposes): [measured in true sonship/ fully like Christ] (obedient and powerfully representing the Kingdom of God) (Eph. 4:12-13).

May the believer's mantra be, "I believe therefore I will now do, and manifest the works of God" (John 3:21; 14:21; James 1:22)." Live yielded and ready for the Master's use.

If this book has been meaningful to you, I'd love to hear about it. You may email your responses to Ekklesiagm@gmail.com.

REFERENCES

All Bible quotations are taken from the Comparative Study Bible, Revised Edition (KJV, AMP, NIV), copyright 1999 by Zondervan; The Holy Bible, New International Version, copyright 1973, 1978, 1984 by International Bible Society; and The Amplified Bible, copyright 1954, 1958, 1962, 1964, 1965, 1987 by Lockman Foundation. (Unless expressly stated KJV is used primarily).

Chapter 1

"Believer." Strong's Definition.

"Believer." Lexico.com, Oxford.

www.lexico.com/dictionary/believer. Accessed 25 Jan. 2021.

"Culture." *Merriam-Webster.com*, Merriam- Webster,

www.merriam- webster.com/dictionary/culture. Accessed 28 Mar. 2018.

REFERENCES

Chapter 2

"Faith." *Merriam-Webster.com*, Merriam-Webster,
www.merriam-webster.com/dictionary/faith.Accessed 18 Mar. 2018.

"Faith." Strong-Lite: H530 & H529 Thayer Definition.

"Faith." Strong's Definition.

"Faith." *The New Strong's Exhaustive Concordance of the Bible: with Main Concordance, Appendix to the Main Concordance, Hebrew and Aramaic Dictionary of the Old Testament, Greek Dictionary of the New Testament*, by James Strong, T. Nelson, 1996, pp. 10–10. Concise Dictionary of the Words in the Hebrew Bible.

"Faith".

Chapter 3

"intimacy." *Dictionary.com Unabridged.* Random House, Inc. Accessed 25 Jan. 2018.<Dictionary.com
http://www.dictionary.com/brows e/intimacy>.

Chapter 4

"Worship." *Dictionary.com Unabridged.* Random House, Inc. Accessed May 20, 2020.<Dictionary.com
http://www.dictionary.com/brows e/worship>.

"Worship." Merriam-Webster.com, Merriam- Webster, www.merriam- webster.com/dictionary/worship. Accessed 20 May. 2020.

"Worship." Strong-Lite: G4352 Thayer Definition.

"Worship." Strong's Definition.

Gumbel, Nicky. "How to Worship God". Aug 17. www.bibleinoneyear.org/bioy/commentary/977

Orr, James, M.A., D.D. General Editor. "Entry for 'Worship'". "International Standard Bible Encyclopedia". 1915.

McGee, J. Vernon. "What Does it Mean to Really Worship?" December 27, 2017. Accessed 19 May 2020.

Chapter 5

"testament." *Dictionary.com Unabridged.* Random House, Inc. Accessed 2 Feb. 2018. <Dictionary.com http://www.dictionary.com/brows e/testament>.

Chapter 6

"Paraclete Definition and Meaning - Bible Dictionary." *Bible Study Tools*, Salem Web Network, www.biblestudytools.com/dictionary/paraclete/. Elwell, Walter A. "Entry for 'Paraclete'". "Evangelical Dictionary of Theology".. 1997.

Orr, James, M.A., D.D. General Editor. "Entry for 'PARACLETE'". "International Standard Bible Encyclopedia". 1915.

"Executor." Lexico.com,

Oxford. www.lexico.com/dictionary/executor. Accessed 8 May. 2020

Chapter 7

"Love." Strong-Lite: G26 Thayer Definition.

"Joy." Strong-Lite: G5479 Thayer Definition.

"Joy." Strong's Definition. "Peace." Strong-Lite: G1515 Thayer Definition "Peace." Merriam-Webster.com, Merriam-Webster, www.merriam-webster.com/dictionary/peace.

Accessed 8 May. 2020.

"Longsuffering." Strong-Lite: G3115 Thayer Definition.

"Gentleness." Strong-Lite: G5544 Thayer Definition.

"Goodness." Strong-Lite: G18 & G19 Thayer Definition.

"Goodness." Strong's Definition.
"Faith." Strong-Lite: G4102 Thayer Definition.

"Faith." Strong's Definition.

"Meekness." Strong-Lite: G4236 Thayer Definition.

"Meekness." Strong's Definition.
"Meekness." Lexico.com, Oxford.

www.lexico.com/dictionary/meekness. Accessed 8 May. 2020.

"Temperance." Strong-Lite: G1466 Thayer Definition.

"Temperance." Strong's Definition.
Chapter 8

"Kingdom." Merriam-Webster.com,

Merriam- Webster, www.merriam-
webster.com/dictionary/kingdom. Accessed 8 May. 2020

Chapter 9

Quote on Satan/serpent
www.biblicalarchaeology.org/daily/biblical-
topics/bible-interpretation/how-the-serpent- became-
satan/

"Serpent." Strong-Lite: H5175 & H5172 Thayer Definition.

Chapter 10

"Administration." Merriam-Webster.com, Merriam- Webster,

www.merriam- webster.com/dictionary/administration. Accessed 8
May. 2020.

REFERENCES

"Operation." Merriam-Webster.com, Merriam- Webster,

www.merriam- webster.com/dictionary/operation. Accessed 8 May. 2020.

"Gift." Merriam-Webster.com, Merriam-Webster,

www.merriam-webster.com/dictionary/gift. Accessed 8 May. 2020.

Hazell, Keith. "Apostles and Prophets – Part 2. 2018.

Caris, Jeremy. "Apostles and Prophets Working

Together". Feb 19, 2015.

"Brutish." Biblestudytools.com. Accessed 16 May

2020.

Burk, Denny. "Is There a Difference between Pastors and Elders". Aug 13, 2019.

Chapter 11

Jones, Jeffrey M. "U.S. Church Membership Down Sharply in Past Two Decades". April 18, 2019.

https://news.gallup.com/poll/248837/church- membership-down-sharply-past-two-decades.aspx

Price, Dr. Paula A. Quotations. "scripturally organic culturally unmodified". 2017.

Chapter 12

"Son." Strong-Lite: G5043 Thayer Definition.

"Son." Strong's Definition.

"Instructor." Strong-Lite: G3807 Thayer Definition.

"Instructor." Strong's Definition.

"Father." Strong-Lite: G3962 Thayer Definition.
"Father." *Dictionary.com Unabridged.* Random House,
Inc. Accessed 17 May 2020. <Dictionary.com
http://www.dictionary.com/brows e/father>.

"Begotten." Strong-Lite: G1080 Thayer Definition.

"Begotten." Strong's Definition.

"Mentor." *Dictionary.com Unabridged.* Random House, Inc. Accessed
17 May 2020. <Dictionary.com http://www.dictionary.com/brows
e/mentor>.

Mattera, Joseph. "Seven Contrasts between Fathers and Teachers."

June 16, 2018. (Blog) www.Josephmattera.org Taylor, David E. 2017.
"Inheritance by Lineage."

Chapter 13

"Occupy." Strong-Lite: G4231 Thayer Definition.

"Tithes." Strong-Lite: H4643

"Tithes." *Dictionary.com Unabridged.* Random House, Inc. Accessed 22 May 2020. <Dictionary.com http://www.dictionary.com/brows e/tithes>.

"First Fruit." Strong-Lite: H7225; G536, G756 Thayer Definition.

"First Fruit." Strong's Definition.

"First Fruit." Merriam-Webster.com, Merriam- Webster,

www.merriam- webster.com/dictionary/first-fruit. Accessed 22 May. 2020

"Offering." Strong-Lite: H8641 Thayer Definition.

"Offering." Strong's Definition.

"Offering." Merriam-Webster.com, Merriam- Webster,

www.merriam- webster.com/dictionary/offering. Accessed 22 May. 2020

"Alms." Merriam-Webster.com, Merriam-Webster,

www.merriam-webster.com/dictionary/alms. Accessed 22 May. 2020

"Honorarium." Merriam-Webster.com, Merriam- Webster,

www.merriam- webster.com/dictionary/honorarium. Accessed 22 May. 2020 Bradley, Jason D.

"20 Bible Verses about Tithing". August 4, 2019. Pushpay

(Significance of Tithing Blog). www.pushpay.com

REFERENCES

About The Author

A true loyalist of the Sovereign Lord, Sadira's intimacy with Him and the spirit realm spans back to her early childhood. Being a prophet from her mother's womb, seeing, hearing, knowing and experiencing God's presence, power and person in her youth has caused her to always manifest exceptional wisdom, knowledge, insights and foresight that extend far beyond her natural experiences and education. In ignorance, as a child, before coming to know she was a prophet, she presumed she may be an angel, seeing it was the only thing that made sense based on how God would use her.

At age 16, once born-again, she began learning, training and being groomed under the tutelage of her foundational father, Ulysses Tuff, an apostle who also operated very strongly in the prophetic. She served in the local ministry for 18 years.

At age 34, she married her husband, Keith Davis, also an apostle of Jesus Christ, who became her covering and father in destiny and purpose.

In April 2008, she was publicly affirmed and prophesied over by Pastor Benny Hinn, who commanded the crowd present and those watching by livestream to remember her face and saying by the Spirit of the Lord, "As a mighty prophet, God will use you to be an example, to be a standard and guidepost in the end-times and like Agabus, you will prophecy the future."

She has been in public ministry for 13 years now and has ministered across the United States, in India and Europe. She has mentored many and ministered to many leaders in various other parts of the world as well, through technology, fortifying their foundations as needed. Additionally, she has done many trainings specifically on the prophetic.

Dedicated to the advancement of the Kingdom of God, restoring purity and honor to the prophet's office, and building the body of Christ in spiritual protocols; soundness in their doctrinal understanding and in their souls (heart, mind, and emotions) is her passion. Being conscientious is second nature, yet her tenderheartedness, tact and genuine love for all humanity has afforded her the opportunity to touch and transform many lives throughout her life from prostitutes and pimps to politicians and preachers. Her nurturing, protective, "motherly" love is often felt in her warm demeanor. Respectively, she is known for her explicit candor and advocacy for truth, righteousness, and justice.

In 2014, she authored and published her first work, the memoir, *A Tale of True Love – Finding Your Mate God's Way.* In 2018, she had the privilege of being a participating author in the published anthology *Junia Arise: Apostolic Women on the Frontlines* with Apostle Axel Sippach. Having received the mantle of a scribe, she has purposed to obey God in writing and publishing many works both in the near and distant future with the purpose of strengthening and supporting the body of Christ. As an apostolic prophet having a global ministry God has plans to use her greatly "for such a time as this" in the earth (Esther 4:14).

Sadira is also a wife and a mother of 7 children, (4 biological and 3 bonus; of which 5 of the 7 are adults), and she has two granddaughters. She currently pastors Ekklesia Global Ministries in Chandler, Arizona.

www.ingramcontent.com/pod-product-compliance
Lightning Source LLC
Chambersburg PA
CBHW060335030426
42336CB00011B/1350